The
Lady with the Lamp
The Story of Florence Nightingale

by Lee Wyndham

Illustrated by Mort Kunstler

D0962939

SCHOLASTIC BOOK SERVICES
NEW YORK • TORONTO • LONDON • AUCKLAND • SYDNEY

This book is sold subject to the condition that it shall not be resold, lent, or otherwise circulated in any binding or cover other than that in which it is published — unless prior written permission has been obtained from the publisher — and without a similar condition, including this condition, being imposed on the subsequent purchaser.

A slightly longer version of this biography is available in hardcover from The World Publishing Company under the title FLORENCE NIGHTINGALE, NURSE TO THE WORLD.

Text copyright © 1970, 1969 by Lee Wyndham. Illustrations copyright © 1970 by Scholastic Magazines, Inc. All rights reserved. Published by Scholastic Book Services, a division of Scholastic Magazines, Inc.

1st printing . . . . March 1970

Printed in the U.S.A.

CONTENTS

Summer at Lea Hurst

Y OUNG FLORENCE NIGHTINGALE gave "Granny" Evans a gentle pat as she walked past the bed to the door of the dingy one-room cottage. In the short time she had today, the girl had tried to set the place to rights. Old Mrs. Evans was nearly helpless now, spending most of her time in bed.

Florence opened the door for a moment. Across the village street she could see her older sister, Parthe, waiting in the open carriage. Parthe sat there, sketching the quaint, thatch-roofed cottages of Papa's tenants. But Parthe would never go inside a cottage to visit, as her mother or Florence did. She said the closed-in smell of the rooms made her ill.

Florence glanced along the street for a sign of her mother. Evidently, Mama was still distributing the jars of broths and jellies she had brought for the tenants.

"Miss Florence? . . ." The frail old woman called uncertainly.

"I'm still here," said Florence. She closed the door and walked back to the bed. "Let's plump up that pillow.

There! Now you can sit up and see the flowers I brought you. And I have some beef broth warming on the stove."

"You're a good kind Miss," Granny Evans said. "And you've grown into a right proper young lady since the last time you were here."

Florence's gray eyes shone, and her delicate skin flushed with pleasure, as she tossed her flowing chestnut hair back from her face. She was slim and tall, and she moved with natural, unhurried grace.

"I am fourteen," Florence told the old woman gravely.

Old Mrs. Evans nodded. Fourteen was a right proper age. At fourteen, the village girls were already working.

"It's a wonder you keep remembering us after being in London and all — and only just come back here for the summer," Granny said.

"But I love it here!" Florence exclaimed, pouring the broth into a big mug. "When we're away, I can hardly wait to get back."

"Back here? To the likes of us?" The old woman's voice rose in astonishment.

"To this very spot," Florence declared. "Drink this," she said, holding the mug close to the aged lips. She stood by patiently, wishing she could do something to really help Granny Evans — and the other poor people in the village. There was so little she could do — so very little. . . .

"There, Miss Florence. I can't take another drop," said the old woman. "I'm that weary."

"See if you can sleep then," Florence suggested. "I'll

look in on you tomorrow. Your granddaughter will be here soon to take care of you, won't she?"

"When she's through at the stocking mill. 'Bout supper time," the old woman replied sleepily.

Florence felt rather than saw the shadow in the doorway. It was her mother, beckoning impatiently. With a last look at Granny Evans, the girl picked up her empty basket and her bonnet, and tiptoed away.

"Really, Flo," her mother began to scold as soon as they were outside. "Can you never keep track of time? Parthe and I have been waiting and waiting for you to get through in there." She hurried Florence into the carriage.

Parthe put away her sketch book as her mother flicked the reins. "I think you like sick people better than well ones," she said to her sister. "I don't see why Mama . . ."

Her words trailed off as the carriage lurched forward. Florence fluffed her bright hair off her neck and immediately her mother said, "Do put your bonnet on, Flo. Your hair is so untidy."

Dutifully Florence slipped on the deep, straw bonnet. Hot, tiresome thing, she thought. Parthe sat beside her, every blonde hair in place, her muslin dress neat and spotless. Parthe almost never displeased Mama. Florence sighed.

"We have guests coming for dinner," Mrs. Nightingale was saying as she urged the horse up the hill. "I really should not have come down to the village today. . . ."

But Florence wasn't really listening. As they drove up the long slope, she was watching for the familiar, breathtaking glimpse of Lea Hurst, the Nightingales' splendid summer home. Mr. Nightingale had designed the house himself. It was built so high on a breezy hill that clouds seemed to brush the roof. The view from the windows was immense. On all sides, the Derbyshire countryside rolled away for miles to the distant blue hills.

Over the *clop, clop* of the horse's hooves, Florence listened for a familiar sound. There it was — the rushing of the Derwent River that flowed between banks of heather below the house. The sound had lulled her to sleep at night ever since she was a little girl.

Florence Nightingale and her sister had been born in Italy, because their wealthy English parents had spent the first three years of married life traveling about in Europe. Parthe had been born in Naples. A year later, on May 12, 1820, Florence was born — in the city of Florence.

Both girls were named after the cities of their birth; Parthenope (Par-then-o-pey) was the Greek name for Naples. But the names were soon shortened. Parthenope became Parthe, or sometimes Pop, and Florence was usually called Flo.

After the young family returned to England, Mr. Nightingale had the great house of Lea Hurst built on a huge estate he had inherited in Derbyshire. Mrs. Nightingale liked living here in the north of England from July to October. Then it became too cold. It was also too far away from the social life of London to suit her.

So Mr. Nightingale bought another even larger house, nearer London, called Embley Park.

As wealthy English families did in the 1800's, the Nightingales traveled from one elegant home to the other — from Lea Hurst to Embley Park — according to the season. Sometimes they visited fashionable seaside resorts or stayed in London.

During these journeys by carriage they often drove through factory towns, and Florence would shudder when she saw the dirty, crowded houses where the workers lived. In London, many of the streets were quite elegant. But the Nightingales' carriage also rumbled through ugly slums. At the sight of the ragged people

and the starving, scarecrow children she saw there, Florence sometimes burst into tears, and then wondered at her sister's calm. "Don't *you* feel sorry for the awful way these people live?" Florence demanded one day.

"Of course," Parthe replied. "But what can *I* do about it? Or *you*, Flo?"

Mrs. Nightingale reached out her gloved hand and patted her younger daughter. "Your father and I do what we can for the people on our own land. As for these miserable city folk — " Mrs. Nightingale shrugged her fur-clad shoulders. "It is sad to think that there must be poor and hungry people in the world. Be thankful that God has blessed *you* with a comfortable home, a mother and father who love you, and a dear sister like Parthe."

Now Florence put her thoughts aside as the carriage whirled into the driveway of Lea Hurst. Her mother handed her the reins. "Drive on to the stable," she directed, "and then come back to the house at once. Both of you. Parthe, see to it that Flo does not linger anywhere! I must wash and change immediately, and you must do the same. . . ." Mrs. Nightingale hurried off, giving directions as she went.

"Hurry up, Flo, do," Parthe said impatiently. "There's so much to be done. I'm to help check the table setting and arrange the flowers for the drawing room. I wish you would learn to do that, Flo. It would please Mama." Florence was always carrying flowers to the villagers, but she would stuff them any old way into Mama's beautiful vases.

Florence moved restlessly. "All that seems so unimportant. I don't want to spend my life arranging flowers and having tea parties and dinner parties, and visits, visits, visits — back and forth — endlessly. I don't see how you and Mama endure it."

"But Flo, that is what we are meant to do. That is what every well brought up young lady is expected to do — until she marries."

"And then?" Florence challenged. "Then it is all to do over again. Sometimes I am so bored that I want to jump up and tell people how I really feel." She ignored her sister's horrified expression and went on, "I even wish we were back at Embley, having lessons with Papa."

Parthe made a face. "Not I. All that history and Latin and Greek and philosophy and languages and mathematics that Papa wants us to learn! I don't see of what use that is to us. And neither does Mama."

But Florence didn't hear. She was remembering how much she enjoyed her lessons with her father. He made all subjects come alive for her. Even the difficult ones, for they were a challenge. Florence liked using her mind. She worked hard at her lessons, while Parthe would escape to her mother as soon as possible. Parthe had grown closer to her mother, while Florence's attachment to her father had deepened.

The girls were at the stable now, and a groom took charge of the horse and carriage.

"I'll only be a moment," Florence said, turning toward the stable door. "I want to see how the pony with the swollen knee is doing."

11

"Oh no you don't!" said Parthe, pulling her sister toward the house. "Have you forgotten what Mama said? No lingering! You and your pets!" she went on. "A pet pony, a pet donkey, a pet nuthatch, a pet *pig!* You try to make a pet of everything. Really, Flo!"

Mrs. Nightingale happened to glance down out of her window as the girls came in sight. She saw clearly who was pulling whom and shook her head ruefully. She could always depend on Parthe — but oh that Florence!

Florence's Secret World

As FLORENCE grew older, she became increasingly "difficult" for her family to understand. Mrs. Nightingale blamed her husband for encouraging Florence in all those studies. The girl had very strange ideas about her social obligations. It was quite proper, of course, for the ladies of the great country houses to be concerned with the welfare of the poor. But Florence actually wanted to *nurse* those people!

She did have a way with the sick. Mrs. Nightingale even encouraged her daughter to help care for various relatives who fell ill or had babies.

"But to nurse *strangers!* How disgusting!" Parthe exclaimed. "What will people think?"

Even Mr. Nightingale, who usually took Florence's side, was alarmed. "She must stop it at once," he insisted. "Where does she get such peculiar ideas?"

Mrs. Nightingale took comfort in one thought. "Soon," she said, "Florence will be going to parties and meeting young men — and that will change her outlook entirely!"

For Florence, the winter when she was sixteen was a most unhappy one. She felt increasingly restless. The family was at Embley Park for the winter season — and here Florence's mother always demanded a great deal more of her socially.

Mrs. Nightingale loved to entertain at Embley Park, and the house was always full of people. It was much larger even than Lea Hurst, which had fifteen bedrooms. And it was a comfortable distance from London. Dozens of the Nightingales' relatives would drive down to visit. Friends and acquaintances, too, often came for a day, a week, or a month. Sometimes whole families arrived for visits — aunts, uncles, a flock of children and babies, and the personal servants.

Mr. Nightingale put up with the constant commotion. But Florence hated it. She was bored with family gossip and preferred to spend her time with the children — amusing the little ones with games, play-acting, and stories — or cuddling the babies whom she loved.

Alone in her room, however, she would pace back and forth, hands clasped tightly together, wondering, *"What are any of us doing that is really important or useful?"*

There was no one with whom Florence could share her troubled thoughts. So she took to writing what she called "private notes," in which she poured out her deepest feelings.

In February, when she was nearly seventeen, Florence had a strange experience, which she recorded in a private note: "On February 7, 1837, God spoke to me and called me to His service." Even as a young girl Florence was deeply religious and often prayed for guidance. The "Voice" she heard then was very real to her, and she was to remember it all her life.

After this experience, Florence was filled with a sense of peace and awareness of her own worth. She felt she had been chosen for an important mission. She did not know what it was — but she was sure that the meaning of the "call" would be revealed to her in time.

When summer came, the Nightingales moved back to Lea Hurst as usual. In spite of her family's disapproval, Florence worked harder than ever among the poor people in the village. She felt closer to understanding what God's "purpose" for her might be when she was caring for the sick.

The idea of nursing as a life work did not enter her mind at that time, although she thought about the public hospitals. In those days, public nursing was not done by young women of Florence's position. Hospital nurses then were considered — and often were — women of such low character that they were not discussed in front of proper young ladies. As for the hospitals — they were filthy pesthouses to which the wretched poor were carted to die when there was no one to care for them. Most people then were nursed at home. Doctors instructed servants or members of the family on proper care. "The thought of going to a hospital is enough to give a respectable body heart failure," the villagers told Florence when she once mentioned the idea.

Florence continued to wonder about hospitals. Why *should* they be so dreadful? Something was terribly wrong. Some day Florence meant to see for herself.

Before she could carry out any such plan, however, her mother announced that the family would travel in Europe. "Going abroad" would put the finishing touches to the girls' education and social accomplishments.

The Nightingales, including Florence, had a splendid time in Europe. They stayed on the continent for a year and a half, visiting famous spots in France, Germany, northern Italy, and Switzerland. They attended concerts, operas, and glittering social events. There were court balls where Grand Dukes and dashing young officers danced attentively with the charming Nightingale sisters. Both girls spoke excellent French, as well as some German and Italian. Florence was especially well read for a young lady of that day. Witty and never at a loss for conversation, she collected admirers wherever she went.

She looked elegant in her Paris costumes and she was a graceful dancer and a lively dinner partner. Mrs. Nightingale sometimes smiled triumphantly at Mr. Nightingale. "See?" her look said plainly. "All that nonsense has blown right out of Flo's head, just as I said it would."

The girl was a brilliant social success, Mama told herself, and would make a brilliant marriage. They must return to England immediately. The girls were old enough to be presented at court now and to be launched into British society.

The prospect of going home shocked Florence. Suddenly she realized that in her enchantment with social life, she had forgotten the Voice that had spoken to her two years before. She had been seeking idle pleasure, instead of preparing herself for her special mission.

In March, before the Nightingales left Paris, Florence wrote a private note in which she resolved to overcome the temptation "to shine in society." The resolve was more easily made than kept. She was surrounded by opportunities "to shine" — and she was eighteen, full of high spirits, and much sought after.

When the Nightingales returned to England in April, Mrs. Nightingale decided they would spend the social season in London.

Once settled in a London hotel, Florence and Parthe were soon caught up in a whirlwind of preparation. To be presented to the Queen was a great social distinction, and everything must go perfectly.

The elegant Nightingale sisters were ushered into the glittering drawing room of Buckingham Palace on May 24, the young Queen Victoria's own birthday. The new Queen was surrounded by her court. When Florence's turn came to be presented, she curtsied deeply. As she rose, her eyes met those of the young Queen. Victoria was twenty. Not much older than myself, Florence thought. Yet Victoria was ruler of the entire British Empire.

The Queen's blue eyes were friendly, interested. She gave Florence a gracious nod and a smile. The presentation was over. Florence, bowing as she stepped carefully backward from the throne, could not know that she and the Queen would meet again at a very different time.

There was a great ball after the presentation, then weeks of fashionable parties followed. Again Florence's "call" grew faint as she moved breathlessly from one gay party to another.

In September 1839, the Nightingales moved back to Embley.

In no time Florence was "at work" among the sick and aged villagers — giving them medicines, making their beds, rubbing their backs and doing goodness knows what else. Mrs. Nightingale was bitterly disappointed, and Parthe joined in her protests. The quarreling at home became unbearable.

There was one person in the family to whom Florence could turn. That was Aunt Mai, her father's sister. Mai (French for May) had given Florence and Parthe their first lessons before she was married. Whenever she could, she would whisk Florence away for a visit.

Now Aunt Mai invited Florence to London. During this visit Florence decided to take up the serious study of mathematics with a tutor — a project that her mother considered utterly ridiculous for a woman, but one that occupied the girl's restless mind and would prove very useful later. When she returned home, Mama and Parthe found Florence more agreeable, though still subject to dark moods of discontent.

"And that in spite of every social success and advantage," Mama complained to a close friend. "I cannot understand the girl. She is gay and witty in society. She could have any number of suitors. And yet she is not happy. Why?"

The answer was that Florence's sensitive nature had always made her painfully aware of two contrasting worlds around her — the comfortable world of the rich and the wretched one of the poor.

England was passing through difficult times. The Industrial Revolution had brought great wealth to some, but to many more it had brought terrible misery. Wages were low. Working conditions in the mills and the factories were hard, but far worse off were the thousands of unemployed. To keep from starving, many stole, and prisons and workhouses were filled to overflowing. This period, known as the "Hungry 1840's," brought especially cruel hardships to the unskilled and ignorant who had no chance of finding work in the factories or of getting the needed training.

It seemed to Florence that too many of her parents' wealthy friends remained untouched by the sufferings around them. Whenever a carriage whisked her to a ball, or a party, to a grand dinner or concert or the opera, she would see groups of ragged and wretched people gathered in the street, looking on as the warmly lit doors swung open to welcome her. The pinched, starved faces and hopeless eyes haunted Florence. Could nothing be done for these unfortunates?

Gradually, she discovered that there *were* others — many of them important people — who were as concerned as she with the suffering of the poor. One was a young man named Richard Monckton Milnes. Florence soon found out that he was not only wealthy, wise, and kind, but also interested in helping young people in trouble with the law.

Florence began to see him often, and her mother was delighted: Richard Milnes was one of the most eligible bachelors in England.

But while Mrs. Nightingale was thinking of an excellent marriage for her daughter, Florence was writing: "My mind is absorbed with the suffering of man. . . . The people I see are eaten up with worry or poverty or disease." As she read her words over, it seemed clear to her that her destiny, her mission, lay among the unfortunate people of the world. Now she felt a step closer to the final revelation of her life's purpose. Then, one day in 1844, she suddenly realized the direction in which she had always been moving.

A Glimpse of the Way

Her life work lay in nursing the sick! Nothing else made her feel so content and useful. But her work must no longer be confined to the village poor, or to her family. It must be on a much larger scale. *She must work in the hospitals.*

Even as a little girl Florence had been a devoted nurse — tending her pets, or her ever-ailing doll family. Or bandaging the broken heads or legs of Parthe's carelessly handled dolls. Florence even made a tiny prescription book for the dolls' medicines — no bigger than a postage stamp — the pages painstakingly sewn together. The medication had been solemnly recommended by an amused family doctor: "powders — 16 grains for an old woman, 11 for a young woman, 7 for a child. . . ." (This tiny evidence of Florence's early interest can be seen in an English museum today.)

Florence knew that she would need a great deal of courage — and wisdom. For her peace of mind, she must have her parents' approval. Yet she could not simply tell them about her resolve. *Hospital* was such a dreadful word in 1844! No, she must plan her approach and bring up the subject to them in exactly the right way.

What arguments could she use to convince them? She had never been inside a hospital. And as for training to be a *nurse* — where could she go? There were no training schools that she knew of. She had never met anyone who had been *taught* how to nurse. The general opinion was that one only needed to be a woman — and willing to care for the sick!

Florence had worked among the sick long enough to know that special knowledge and skills were required. How often had she stood helplessly, unable to relieve suffering. *No, tenderness and sympathy were not enough.* A nurse should know the effect of disease on the body and be aware of advances in medicine. Only then could she carry out intelligently the orders of the doctors. (This idea, so obvious to Florence, was in fact revolutionary for her time — not only in England, but everywhere else in the world, including the United States.)

Not far from Embley there was a well-known hospital, the Salisbury Infirmary. The head physician was Dr. Fowler, an old family friend. Florence went to him with her plan to *study* nursing.

At first, Dr. Fowler did not believe that Florence was serious. To test her, he took her through the hospital himself. "It won't take you long to change your mind," he said.

Entering a ward, Florence was almost overcome by

the terrible stench. Quickly she raised her handkerchief to her nose.

Dr. Fowler smiled ruefully. "That's what is commonly known as 'hospital smell,' Florence. It is a combination of dirt, diseased flesh, and poor sanitation. Have you had enough?"

With an effort, Florence mastered her mounting nausea. "We have only begun," she said, and forced herself to look about. "Are the floors and walls never washed?"

"Oh yes, when we can get men to do it. We have the walls limed — to kill the smell. The workmen who do this often become ill themselves. It is not a popular task."

Why the men fell ill was not investigated. The effects of germs and bacteria, and how infections are spread were not part of medical knowledge then. The use of antiseptics was still twenty years away.

"Isn't it possible to let in some fresh air? To open a window?" Florence asked.

"As you can see, the only source of heat in this ward is that single fire at the far end. In cold weather our windows must be kept closed for warmth."

Florence gazed over the crowded room. There were at least fifty beds in here, less than two feet apart. The sheets and blankets were filthy. Most of the patients looked miserable and neglected.

"These are the difficult conditions under which we doctors must work," Dr. Fowler said. "Now that you have seen them, surely you will change your mind about nursing."

But Florence was more determined than ever. Something *had* to be done to improve these horrible wards.

"Where are the nurses?" she asked.

At that moment a coarse, dirty woman with a puffy face plodded into the ward. She bent over a patient, poked him roughly and said something to him in a hoarse, grating voice.

The color drained out of Florence's face, then flooded back in indignation. She turned toward Dr. Fowler, but he had his arm under her elbow and was leading her away from the ward.

"That is our worst problem of all," he told her. "The women willing to work as nurses are untrained and uneducated. Some can neither read nor write. Many are always drunk. That's why they can't find jobs as kitchen maids — in far easier, pleasanter surroundings. And some — " Dr. Fowler stopped himself and coughed delicately. "In short," he said, "it would be unthinkable for a young lady like yourself to associate with such women."

Florence's gaze did not waver. "It is even more unthinkable to me that the poor and helpless sick must suffer for lack of proper care," she said quietly.

Dr. Fowler was impressed by her attitude. But he much doubted that she would have the strength to carry through her remarkable aim to do hospital nursing. Reluctantly he agreed to help her with her "training" — if she could get her parents' consent.

She chose to make her announcement while Dr. Fowler and his wife were visiting the Nightingales for the holidays.

"Mama, Papa, you both know that I have always been interested in caring for the sick. Now Dr. Fowler has consented to supervise my training at Salisbury Hospital for a period of three months so that I can be a real nurse. With your permission," she said earnestly, "I should like to begin immediately after the holiday season."

Florence had expected her family to oppose the idea. But she was not prepared for the stark horror in her mother's face.

Her father was speechless. Parthe began to sob. Mrs. Fowler, who had been told of Florence's plans, looked as if she wished she were somewhere else.

"Florence!" Her elegant, beautiful, always proper mother shrieked. "Do you want to disgrace yourself and your family?"

Then Mr. Nightingale found his voice. "Dr. Fowler, how can you have encouraged such madness?" he demanded.

Florence turned pale. She had counted on Dr. Fowler to support her. But now the embarrassed doctor admitted that the plan "presented serious difficulties." Of course Florence must abandon it. He would not look at the girl's stricken face.

Florence was convinced that what she wanted to do was right. But she was bitterly disappointed, and sick in heart and mind. It seemed that there was no one who could help her, nowhere to turn.

The Nightingale household was in an uproar for days. But they still had social engagements to keep. Dinners and visits were farthest from Florence's thoughts, but she had to accompany her mother and Parthe on these occasions and be "witty and merry."

Strangely, by turning to social affairs she took a giant step toward her goal of training to become a nurse.

At one gathering she met a sympathetic young lord and told him of her interest in improving conditions in hospitals. "But I do not know enough about the subject," she confessed, "and Mama will not hear of my going near a hospital."

"Then the hospitals must come to you," the young

lord said decisively. "You must study the Blue Books and hospital reports. In that way you will learn what is wrong and can consider what might be done. I shall have some sent to you at once."

And so Blue Books, government publications dealing with public health, sanitation, and conditions among the poor, were sent to her. The material required careful, thoughtful study — and secrecy. If her mother had known what Florence was reading, she would have burned all of them.

Florence got up before dawn and worked by candlelight, wrapped in a shawl, for she did not dare light a fire in her fireplace. She filled notebook after notebook

with details so that she could compare facts and figures. She wrote to hospitals all over England for more information and to important people she had met in Germany and France during her family's tour abroad. She compared the information they sent her with the situation in England. Now she learned that there were Catholic orders that trained nuns for nursing. Why, she wondered, was there no nursing training for those outside the Catholic church?

Meanwhile, her brilliant mind sorted and stored every new fact. Eventually her studies would make her a world authority on hospitals. For now this was an all-absorbing interest that eased her frustration.

When the breakfast bell rang, she put away her charts and notebooks, smoothed her hair, brushed out her clothes, and went downstairs to the family.

It was in October when Florence received an important book from no less an important person than the Prussian Ambassador. It was the *Yearbook of the Lutheran Deaconesses of Kaiserswerth*. Kaiserswerth was a little German town on the Rhine where the Lutheran Pastor Fliedner ran an orphanage, hospital, and school for the training of Protestant deaconesses to nurse the sick.

Florence read of their work and training with growing excitement. These people were not nuns bound by sacred vows, but simply good women with a dedication to relieve suffering.

This was the place for her! On October 7, 1846, she wrote a private note, "There is my home, there are my brothers and sisters all at work. There my heart is, and there, I trust, will one day be my body."

But in spite of her own convictions, there were many problems to solve, many decisions to be made, before Florence could think of undertaking the training at Kaiserswerth. One problem in particular occupied her thoughts.

A Fateful Meeting

SHOULD SHE marry Richard Milnes?

He had been courting Florence for years. He was sympathetic to what he knew of her dreams, for he was kind and charitable. Florence could well imagine that life would be wonderful with a man like Richard.

But how could she marry Richard and hope to carry through her work in hospitals? He would want a wife who was completely devoted to him, who could enter happily into his social life, and be a mother to his children. And this would mean renouncing her mission, which she could not do. But neither could she bear to send Richard away forever.

Florence's mother became impatient, then angry with her indecision. She accused her daughter of being ungrateful, of not appreciating her good fortune in having Richard's love. What on earth was she waiting for?

The strain of Florence's own indecision, and the constant nagging of her family, finally brought Florence close to a nervous collapse. Suddenly everyone was worried about her. A trip abroad was suggested. Selina and Charles Bracebridge, who were good friends of the family, were to spend the winter in Rome. Why not take Florence with them?

Selina understood Florence. So along with the visits to art galleries, palaces, and churches, Florence visited hospitals and orphanages too. She studied the work done by Catholic sisters in these institutions. Florence did not mention these visits in her letters home. But she filled her private notebooks with the useful facts she learned.

In Rome Florence met a handsome young couple — Liz and Sidney Herbert. Mr. Herbert was a distinguished statesman, with an important position in the government.

Neither the Herberts nor Florence could know how closely their lives would soon be linked together. But they liked each other immediately and so they met frequently to talk and go sightseeing together.

One of the things that drew them together was Sidney Herbert's interest in hospital reform. He was building a small rest home himself, on his estate in England. Here working people who had been discharged from hospitals could stay and regain their strength before returning to their jobs. Such a thing was almost unheard of in those days. Florence was eager to know more, to see the plans for the buildings, to learn how the place would be run and the people cared for.

Later, when she had returned to England, Florence visited the Herberts. There she met other people who were also interested in hospital reform, and she impressed them with her remarkable knowledge of hospitals.

Mrs. Nightingale was pleased by Florence's friendship with the wealthy and important Herberts. She had no idea, of course, that they approved of Florence's ambition to study nursing, and of her plan to go to Kaiserswerth.

While Florence was turning over in her mind the ways and means of getting to Kaiserswerth, Richard Milnes insisted on an answer. Would she or would she not marry him? He had to know. Now. Florence refused him. She *had* to — for his sake as well as her own.

Mrs. Nightingale was more than disappointed — she was furious. Parthe wept over what she felt was madness on her sister's part. Mr. Nightingale became disgusted with all this female hysteria and took himself off to London.

Florence felt crushed and defeated. Had she made the right decision? Had she given Richard up for a dream that would never come true?

The constant quarreling at home wore her down. She felt tired, uncertain, tearful. Sometimes she fainted during the nagging family "discussions."

Selina Bracebridge again came to the rescue. She and her husband were going to Egypt and Greece. Would Mrs. Nightingale permit Florence to go with them?

Although traveling through Egypt and Greece should have been exciting, Florence remained pale and listless. But now Selina knew what was wrong. She learned of Florence's passion to visit Kaiserswerth, and she and her husband were determined that Florence should go there.

They would return home by way of Germany, she told Florence. She and her husband would spend two weeks in Dusseldorf, and Florence could go on to Kaiserswerth, only six miles away.

Florence had dreamed for so long of this opportunity. She could scarcely believe that she was actually going, at last. Then she grew frightened. What would her mother and father say? But when the Bracebridges arranged for her to visit some hospitals and charitable institutions in Berlin, Florence forgot her qualms.

At Kaiserswerth she was welcomed by Pastor Fliedner and his wife. Eagerly she inspected the hospital, observed the deaconesses at work, and the condition of the children in the orphanage.

She left on August 13, 1850, "feeling so brave as if nothing could vex me again," she wrote. She would return as soon as proper arrangements could be made for her to begin her training. Surely there would be no more objections at home. She was filled with love for her family, certain of their approval and understanding.

She arrived at Lea Hurst on August 21, in high spirits. There was a loving reunion with her family. But when they heard of her visit to Kaiserswerth, Mrs. Nightingale was furious.

Florence had behaved shamefully. She was never to mention Kaiserswerth again. She would be forced to behave dutifully, to stay at home and engage in the life proper to her upbringing and station.

Within a few weeks Florence felt broken in spirit. In January 1851, she wrote, "What is to become of me? . . . Why can't I be satisfied with the life that satisfies so many people? . . . What am I to do?"

In April she was able to get away from her family and visit the Herberts at their estate in Wilton. Immediately she felt refreshed by their friendship, approval, and interest. Among the guests there she met an astonishing young woman — *Doctor* Elizabeth Blackwell, the first woman to be granted a medical degree in the United States! How had she ever managed to break through the ironclad traditions? The fact that she had done so strengthened Florence's sagging courage. She could not hear enough of Dr. Blackwell's experiences.

When Florence returned to Embley, she brought Dr. Elizabeth Blackwell with her. Mrs. Nightingale was startled by their guest's title — and not at all reassured by her experiences in the hospital world. Florence caught her mother watching Dr. Elizabeth as if she couldn't imagine how the young woman had managed to remain a lady — after all *that*.

Florence's friendship with Elizabeth Blackwell, the glimpse of Kaiserswerth, which her good friends the Bracebridges had arranged, and the encouragement of the Herberts, all served to alter her attitude toward her family. "I have been so long treated as a child," she wrote in her diary, "and have so long allowed myself to be treated as a child. . . . Now I am thirty-one. . . . Now no more childish things, no more vain things, no more love, no more marriage. Now, Lord, let me only think of Thy will."

On June 8, 1851, she set down her decision to leave home and take up her studies. "I must expect no sympathy or help from them," she wrote, "I must *take* some things, as few as I can to enable me to live. I must *take* them; they will not be given to me."

Two weeks later she arranged to go to Kaiserswerth to study for three months. This time, no arguments, no tears, no scenes had the slightest effect on Florence. Her mother finally faced the fact that her daughter was leaving — with or without her consent.

"Very well," she said. "But you will leave my way. Everything must be done in secret for the sake of your family. You can see for yourself how ill Parthe is — worrying over you. We shall say that she has been ordered to go to Carlsbad for a three-month cure. We shall leave together, and you can go on — to *that* place, then rejoin us, and we'll come home together. You are to tell no one about it. No one."

"But the Herberts know," Florence pointed out. "And the Bracebridges, and Aunt Mai."

"You are to tell no one else then," Mrs. Nightingale insisted. "You are not to write people from *that* place. Do you understand, Florence?"

Her mother went on and on until her father finally stalked out of the drawing room. He too was disappointed in their daughter, but he found the eternal bickering unbearable. He refused to go with his family to Carlsbad, and shut himself up in his library, with his books.

For Florence, the trip was a painful one. There were constant complaints and arguments with her mother and sister. Even on Florence's last night in Carlsbad she was given no peace. "My sister," wrote Miss Nightingale years later, "threw my bracelets which I offered her to wear, in my face, and the scene which followed was so violent that I fainted."

But Florence triumphed at last. On the following evening she reached her goal — Kaiserswerth.

Kaiserswerth

FLORENCE NIGHTINGALE's carriage drew to a stop at Kaiserswerth, and the driver helped her down. The exhausting journey from England, yesterday's bitter quarrel, the bad night's sleep, all were forgotten. Trembling with excitement, Florence watched two women in blue uniforms, with crisp white caps and aprons, approach her.

"Welcome, Miss Nightingale. Welcome back to Kaiserswerth," they said.

Florence gave the deaconesses a radiant smile. "I can't tell you how happy I am to be back," she said.

Florence had hoped to see Pastor Fliedner in the morning and to start her duties immediately. But he did not summon her to his study until the afternoon. She had liked him immensely on her first visit to Kaiserswerth. But now she was no longer a guest. Florence sensed that now he was passing judgment on her, weighing her character and sincerity of purpose.

Miss Nightingale was different from the deaconesses he had trained, the Pastor thought. They were peasant women, used to hard, backbreaking labor. This young woman was of a very different social class, accustomed to a worldly, luxurious life. Would she resent the lowly tasks? Would she last more than a week under the strict discipline at Kaiserswerth?

He said, "I am glad that you have returned to us, Miss Nightingale. We lead a simple life here — but a rewarding one."

Life was indeed simple at Kaiserswerth, and it was hard too. Florence rose at five o'clock. Forty-five minutes later she was eating a breakfast of plain, peasant food. Next, the children at the orphanage had to be fed and dressed. Then Florence went with the deaconesses to the hospital, where a hundred patients had to be cared for. How different they looked from those poor souls she remembered in Salisbury Hospital in England!

The hospital at Kaiserswerth was scrupulously clean. No patients were neglected, and most of them were even cheerful despite their illness. The sisters did their work efficiently and well, and with deep sympathy for their patients. Unlike ordinary nurses of the day, these women were good, simple people. They were dedicated to their work, and they cared for the sick with loving attention.

Soon Florence was carrying trays and helping to move patients. She washed them, combed their hair, and made their beds. Then she was taught to change dressings and give them medicines. Her hands were swift and gentle, her voice soft, her smile bright and encouraging.

"She makes me believe that I'll get well," a shadowy little woman whispered to the patient next to her.

Florence soon discovered that the cleanliness and order in the hospital did not come about by magic. The deaconesses were assigned the tasks of washing, dusting, and scrubbing the floors.

The most difficult task Florence had ever had to do at home was to keep an accurate count of her mother's silver and linens. Now, when her turn came, she knelt beside the sisters and scrubbed floors as hard as any of them. They scarcely had time to eat — only ten minutes for each meal.

Yet Florence found such new zest and happiness in this busy life, she could not bear not to share it. Her mother had said to write to no one. But surely that did not mean she did not want to hear from her own daughter.

In July 1851, Florence wrote her mother. "I find the deepest interest in everything here, and am so well in body and mind . . . I know you will be glad to hear this, dearest Mum . . . Until yesterday I never even had time to send my things to the wash . . . I wish for no other world but this . . ."

Florence soon began to feel, however, that she was not learning enough about nursing as a *profession*. All she really was doing was helping to keep patients comfortable. She was disappointed to find that there were no classes in hygiene, no real study of disease and illness. In fact, there was no great variety of disease among the patients at Kaiserswerth. In big city hospitals one could study disease. That would have to come later. But now she must get every bit of training available here. She decided to speak to Pastor Fliedner about an assignment to more serious duties where she could do more and observe more.

When she entered his study, she thought that he regarded her with disappointment. Surely this could not be because her work was unsatisfactory?

"Yes, Miss Nightingale. What is it you wish?" he asked, motioning her to be seated.

Eagerly, Florence said, "I want to learn all I can about nursing all kinds of cases. I have been present at deathbeds and at difficult births in our village and among the members of my family. Now, with your permission, I would like to observe operations and learn what I can about taking care of such patients."

"My dear Miss Nightingale!" Before she finished, Pastor Fliedner was on his feet — beaming. "I had no idea — I expected — I was certain you had come to announce your intention to leave Kaiserswerth."

It was Florence's turn to be surprised. "*Leave!* Now? I wouldn't dream of it! My days here have been the happiest of my life. Besides . . ."

Pastor Fliedner finally had to hold up his hand to silence her enthusiasm. "Your request is granted," he told Florence, smiling.

In 1851 operating methods were crude. Antiseptics — to prevent infection — were still unknown. Anesthetics

— which relieved pain or put the patient to sleep — had only recently been discovered. Patients were strapped to operating tables and held by strong men. Doctors had to steel themselves against the terrible screams of the patients. Instruments used on one patient were often immediately used on the next without cleansing. Later, Florence realized how dreadful this was, but at that time she accepted the practice without question.

She was near fainting at those first operations she witnessed. But she fixed her mind on the thought that whatever was being done was necessary to save the patient's life.

In letters to her mother she skipped the gruesome details, but she did mention being present at several operations, including an amputation of a workman's leg. Her mother was disgusted, her sister horrified.

In August, the Herberts visited Florence, and Pastor Fliedner told them that "no person had ever passed so distinguished an examination, or shown herself so thoroughly mistress of all she had to learn as Miss Nightingale."

Florence stayed at Kaiserswerth nearly four months. When she joined her mother and sister at Cologne, she was greeted coldly.

Parthe was as irritable as ever. "I do hope you are satisfied, Florence. I have not been able to sleep well since you left. I was simply *haunted* by the thought of the disgusting things you were doing."

"Surely now you have had enough of this mad idea of

public nursing," her mother added. "Look at your hands! They are more fitting to a common drudge. You must wear gloves until they heal again, so people will not see them. When we return to England, let us have no more of these disgraceful whims of yours."

Florence pressed her lips together and said nothing. Argument, she knew now, was useless. But for her, Kaiserswerth was only a beginning. There was so much more she must learn about nursing — and she intended to learn it. There were big hospitals in London, Dublin, Paris. She would visit them all. As soon as she returned home she would begin to make the necessary arrangements. She would use the influence of her friends.

An unpleasant surprise awaited the Nightingales when they returned to Embley, and Florence had to postpone her plans. They found Mr. Nightingale resting quietly in a darkened room. Downstairs his study was closed. For weeks he had not been able to read or write.

"I'm afraid I am losing my eyesight," he told his wife and daughters.

"What do the doctors say?" Mrs. Nightingale fluttered around him helplessly. "Surely something can be done!" Her husband had never been ill before and she was terrified.

"We can go back to Carlsbad," suggested Parthe. "The mineral waters there are supposed to do wonders. You will be well there in no time."

Mr. Nightingale sighed and shook his head. It was clear he had almost given up hope.

Flo examined her father's inflamed eyes. He was obviously suffering much pain.

"Have the doctors advised you? Didn't you see an oculist?" she asked gently.

Mr. Nightingale admitted that he had. "He wants me to go to Umberslade. I must take the cold-water treatments there, he says."

"Why haven't you gone, Papa?" Florence cried.

"I don't want to go, Flo. Not unless you will come with me. I don't want any other nurse."

"But of course Flo will go with you," Mrs. Nightingale put in quickly. "It will be a fine opportunity for her to devote some of her nursing skill to her own family. Who has a better right to it?"

She gave her daughter an angry look. Flo sighed. Even at a time like this her mother could not forget her bitterness.

Florence knelt beside her father's chair. "I'll gladly go with you, Papa," she assured him. "Please do not worry. I shall be at your side whenever you need me."

Florence and her father left for Umberslade within the week. There Mr. Nightingale's sight improved gradually. Florence read to him, walked with him, talked with him. The closeness she had once known with her father returned. At last she felt free to confide in him.

"I do not want to hurt you or Mama. But I cannot live the life you have planned for me. I must do what I feel is right for me," she told him.

"And what you feel is right for you is to go out among the wretched poor as a nurse?" he asked her gently.

Florence nodded.

"Oh my dear, what a hard life you have chosen! I cannot bear to think of it."

"Please, Papa. It is what I want, what I *must* do. Help me! As long as I live at home Mama and Parthe will try to stop me. You have heard the arguments. It makes us all miserable. I must be free."

Florence told her father what had happened at Carlsbad and on her trip home — and of her happiness in the work at Kaiserswerth.

Papa said nothing, but he held Florence close for a moment and kissed the top of her head. Florence's mother and sister had treated her badly. For the first time he seemed fully aware of his younger daughter's wretchedness. He must find a way to help her. She had suffered enough.

"Leave me now, Florence," he told her tenderly. "I must give this matter some thought."

When Mr. Nightingale finally came to a decision, everyone was surprised. His wife was furious, but there was nothing she could do about it. Mr. Nightingale had arranged for Florence to have an income of her own. With this money she could now live away from home, as she wished.

Florence began to make plans at once. In April 1853, she arranged to go as a student to the hospital managed by the Sisters of Charity in Paris. She was actually packing her bags when a letter from Liz Herbert caused her to alter her plans.

The Lady Superintendent

F LORENCE read and reread Liz Herbert's letter with mounting excitement. "I have heard of a suitable position for you," Liz wrote. "It will require all your talents for nursing, organization, and diplomacy. . . ."

The opening was in a small private nursing home — not an ordinary hospital — called The Institution for the Care of Sick Gentlewomen in Distressed Circumstances. Here, ladies with little or no money, and no relatives or friends to look after them were cared for. Many of them were governesses or paid "companions." This was the only kind of work considered respectable enough for a lady who needed to earn her living.

It was unthinkable for such people to be forced to go into the dreadful London hospitals. So this project became a favorite charity of prominent society ladies. But it had gotten into difficulties because of poor management.

Now it was planned to move the institution from its present location and reorganize it completely. Liz Herbert had heard the news from her friend, Lady Canning, who was chairman of the committee and responsible for finding a superintendent to manage the institution. Liz had at once recommended Florence, who would hear directly from Lady Canning in a few days. Florence could scarcely wait.

When the letter came, she was thrilled with the position it described, and a meeting was quickly arranged.

Lady Canning's manner at the interview was regal and very formal. Florence could not tell if she was approved of or not.

"What we need, Miss Nightingale, is a capable person who can supervise the alterations of our new home. Afterward this person would have the responsibility of running the entire institution." Lady Canning paused and looked at Florence critically. "I hope you will forgive me for saying so, but you seem rather young for such a post. We had in mind a more mature person."

Florence smiled politely — and she hoped, confidently. But she was anxious. How much she could do in a position like this! If only they would accept her! She did her best to impress Lady Canning with her vast knowledge of hospital organization. But her youthfulness for such a position could not be talked away. Was she to be denied this chance to put into practice all that she learned? As if she were so young that she needed a chaperon! Of course! That was the solution.

"Suppose I bring with me a superior, elderly, highly respectable person — as matron or housekeeper," Florence suggested. "Would that be agreeable to the committee?"

Lady Canning looked doubtful. "I am afraid the committee would not care to add wages for such a person to its other expenses."

Florence was relieved. At least this would not be a problem.

"I would be happy to hire the housekeeper and pay her wages myself," she offered.

Lady Canning seemed pleased with this arrangement. But the committee must be consulted.

Florence was kept waiting several weeks. There were more interviews with the full committee of ladies — and more questions.

"Would it be proper for a lady like Miss Nightingale to nurse women of a lower class?"

"Was it proper for a lady to be present at medical examinations?"

Like Parthe and her mother, many of the ladies on the committee were shocked to learn that Miss Nightingale had already been present at such examinations and had actually observed operations.

Florence's quiet sensible manner, her obvious store of knowledge, and her personal charm and tact finally triumphed. By the end of April 1853, the position was hers.

She was to work without pay, as befitted her social station. The expenses of the matron would be met by her also. However, she was to have complete control and management of the institution and all its funds. Florence was quite satisfied with this arrangement.

Her duties would not begin until the new building was found, and this would be a matter of several weeks. Not one to waste time, Florence decided to resume her journey to Paris — and her intended studies with the Sisters of Charity.

Again her mother and Parthe objected hysterically. A hospital was still a hospital, even if it was called a nursing home. Florence was disgracing them again. Since Mama could do nothing about Flo's "going into service," she could see no reason for her daughter's jaunt to Paris to study at *another* hospital. Surely she could spend these last few weeks in the company of her mother and sister.

This Florence would not do.

She went abroad armed with a special permit to visit any hospitals she chose. So before reporting for her training with the sisters, she made a number of inspection tours. She also talked to famous Paris doctors and surgeons and watched them at work in their clinics.

Then she reported to the Sisters of Charity. All went well for two weeks — and then she came down with the measles! That was the end of her "training" in any hospital as a student. For she never again had time for this kind of study. All that she knew, and was to put into practice to save lives and ease pain, she learned from reading, observation, and her own actual experience in dealing with the sick.

Florence was able to return to London in mid-July. During the month that followed, she had Aunt Mai's help in supervising the alterations of the new house chosen for the institution. And what magnificent plans Florence had for it!

"We shall want hot water piped to every floor," she told the committee.

"Think of the expense!" cried Lady Canning. "The nurses can fetch the water from one floor to another."

Florence remained firm. "Nurses who have to run about fetching hot water become merely pairs of legs. A nurse should not have to leave her floor or her patients while on duty."

The committee gave its approval. Pipes were to be installed as Miss Nightingale directed.

This was only the beginning. Lady Canning's committee were soon examining "windlass installations" — small boxlike elevators — in various buildings in the city.

"Food and supplies can be lifted from floor to floor by this rope and pulley device," Florence explained. "This will save the nurses time and work."

The small and very handy "elevators" were installed. But there seemed to be no end to Miss Nightingale's unusual demands.

"Each patient should be able to ring for the nurse," she said. "Bells should ring in the passage outside the nurse's door. But they should be a special kind of bell. Each one should have a valve — a little hinged lid — that will fly open and stay open."

"Whatever for?" asked the ladies. "Isn't one ordinary bell enough to summon the nurse?"

"An ordinary bell would not tell the nurse which patient has rung," Florence explained. "If the valve remains open, she can give prompt attention to the woman who has rung."

It did seem logical. And so the new bells were also installed.

Although there was some grumbling in the committee about Miss Nightingale's strange new ideas, many were pleased. Theirs would be an up-to-date institution, a model of its kind.

In August, Florence decided to move with her matron, Mrs. Clarke, into the new home of the institution, at No. 1 Harley Street. Then she could be certain that all her orders were carried out.

During her very first week there, Florence and the committee had a serious argument. Lady Canning and several others arrived early one morning. Florence met them in her private sitting room. As they stormed in, Lady Canning waved the list of prospective patients in front of Florence.

"What is the meaning of this, Miss Nightingale?" she demanded angrily. "Here!" She pointed to a name on the list.

Florence replied calmly. "It is the name of one of our new patients. Surely you do not expect me to consult the committee each time a new patient applies for admission?"

"That is not the point," interrupted one of the ladies. "This woman is not a member of the Church of England! She is a Roman Catholic. We have never accepted anyone in the institution who was not of our faith."

"You will have to send her somewhere else," Lady Canning said firmly.

Florence's gray eyes glowed with anger. Did the ladies really imagine that only women of their own faith were worthy of medical aid? How cruel and narrow-minded! For a moment she could not trust herself to speak. When she did, her voice was icy.

"Very well, if that is what you wish. I will send her somewhere else. But then I must bid you good morning. I will begin packing my things at once. If the institution means to turn away sick and helpless women on the basis of religion, I too must leave."

Regardless of how much she wanted this position, Florence refused to be a party to such prejudice.

The ladies were taken by surprise. The institution was to open in a few days. Where could they find another competent director? Miss Nightingale could not leave now! Florence was unmoved. Either the institution was to be opened to all who were in need, or she would leave. The ladies looked at each other helplessly. They *needed* Florence — and so they agreed to her terms.

By autumn the institution was filled with patients. The Lady Superintendent seemed to be everywhere at once, managing nurses — the best decent women she could find — assisting at operations, and often nursing difficult patients herself.

Her devotion to her duties — to the smallest detail — was felt throughout the hospital. If the coal cellar needed checking, Florence went down and checked. Cupboards and storerooms were turned out and examined. Lists were made of things they had and longer lists of things they needed.

At one point Florence discovered that the ladies on the committee had bought a small quantity of very expensive jam. On the other hand, they had neglected to order the brushes and brooms and dusters she had requested. After that Florence attended to the ordering herself. As for the jam, perhaps she recalled making pots and pots of it at her mother's insistence. Now she had the kitchen staff make the jam at a fraction of the cost of buying it. The committee ladies were impressed by the saving.

Because Florence was on her feet a good part of the day and night, she wrote to Embley, asking her mother for a pair of comfortable old boots. And, since the committee had by now spent all its money, Florence also appealed to her family for linen, carpets, curtains, and food for the patients.

Mrs. Nightingale could not approve of her daughter's life. But she was becoming resigned to it. She began to respond to Florence's requests. Odd pieces of linen were sewn together. Old curtains were made into bed covers. Florence's patients were provided with clean sheets and patched rugs as well as good food. Hampers of flowers, fruit, vegetables, and meat began to arrive for the patients every week.

Parthe came around more slowly. After some coaxing, she agreed to have tea with Florence in her sitting room at Harley Street. But then as she entered the institution, she had hysterics and collapsed.

In spite of the problems which inevitably arose in her work, Florence was still able to write, in January 1854, "I have never repented nor looked back, not for one moment. And I begin the New Year with more true feeling of a happy New Year than I ever had in my life."

The ladies on the committee were pleased with the work Miss Nightingale was doing — even those who had opposed her ideas. Her talent for organizing herself and those she worked with, and the tact with which she handled people, had won them over. Florence could be sweet, womanly, and gentle, but she could also be icily firm — and she knew just when and on whom to use these tactics.

Her patients adored her. She was never too busy to listen to their problems and their secret fears. Many times she helped her "gentlewomen in distressed circumstances" even after they had left the institution. One of the patients was a governess who had been ill for many weeks. When it was time for her to leave the institution, she was still weak. Florence learned that she intended to take a position immediately.

"You are not well enough to work," she told the

woman. "You must rest or you will be back here within a month."

The woman looked helplessly at her. "I *must* work, Miss Nightingale. I have no money. I cannot afford a rest."

Immediately Florence arranged to send the governess to the country at her own expense.

When she was completely well, the governess wrote Florence a long and grateful letter. "I cannot thank you enough for this extra rest, my dear, dear Miss Nightingale. I cannot even express how much indebted I am to you."

There were many such letters to Miss Nightingale from poor and friendless women whom she helped.

Florence's father was now a county official, and one of his responsibilities was the management of hospitals and asylums. He and Florence wrote each other frequently, and Mr. Nightingale followed his daughter's work with great interest — and pride.

He sympathized with her ordeals. And he was amused by the manner in which she got her way with the committee. Now and then he was even awed by the huge savings she managed on the purchase of drugs or food for her patients.

He was the one she wrote to when things went wrong — when a heavy gas stove chimney came down and "would certainly have killed a patient," if Florence had not been there to catch it in her arms! Or when a drug was sent with a wrong label. The patient would have been poisoned, "if I had not smelt it before it was given to her," Florence wrote him.

Although Florence was often worried and depressed by her patients' problems, her friends did not know it. Through the years she had learned to mask her feelings. She remained a cheerful companion and a charming guest. Her popularity never waned, and social invitations were frequently delivered by hand to her Harley Street apartment. One said: "Lock up your ladies, leave someone else to stir the gruel, and cab round to me." And when she could, Florence did just that.

Mrs. Nightingale had been certain that the life her daughter had chosen would be frowned upon by London society, but she was wrong. Many people admired the work she was doing, and Florence was invited everywhere. She felt especially close to Liz Herbert, who had suggested her for this position. The Herberts were as interested in hospital reform as Florence was. And Sidney Herbert was in a position to do something about it, for he had a great deal of influence in the government.

Florence had been the director of the institution for almost a year now. Things were running so smoothly that she was becoming restless. There must be more she could do. Something in Florence never allowed her to feel she was doing enough.

In May, Liz Herbert wrote her that Sidney wanted information about hospital nurses, their poor pay and worse lodging. If he had enough material, he might be able to get some of the evils remedied.

Florence set about gathering this material immediately.

She found the facts as disturbing as ever. The years had brought no improvements in the London hospitals. Nurses still "slept in wooden cages on the landing places outside the doors of the wards . . . where it was impossible for the night nurse taking her rest in the day to sleep at all, owing to the noise, where there was no light or air."

Under such conditions, how could hospitals hope to get decent women to serve as nurses?

Each nurse was expected to care for a large number of patients. In one case, Miss Nightingale discovered a single nurse in charge of four wards — well over two hundred patients.

As for the "care" given the sick — the patients came in filthy from the London slums and remained that way. "The nurses as a general rule did not wash patients." The beds smelled even worse than the poor wretches in them. Their meals were greasy messes. Even water was not taken around — unless the nurse happened to remember to do it.

A doctor in a large London hospital told Florence that there were only two nurses whom the surgeons could trust to give medicine to their patients. And a head nurse of another large institution said that in the course of her large experience she "had never known a nurse who was not drunken."

Of course the "nice" people — the ladies and the gentlemen — knew that hospitals for common folk were not *quite* what they should be. As for the nurses, "Surely they weren't as bad as all *that*," one of the titled ladies was reported saying. "And if they do drink a little . . . poor people, it must be so tiresome sitting up all night."

But could a better type of nurse be found?

When Liz Herbert called at Harley Street to discuss this problem, Florence told her friend, "The 'nurses' are considered a necessary horror. If that is the way people feel, the situation will never improve."

Flo held up a letter from a doctor she had met in Paris. "This poor man asks me to recommend two reliable, skillful nurses to act as matrons. Alas, I know of no such marvels."

Liz frowned. "But there must be a way to produce such nurses. The more that people hear about good nurses, the more they will want them. *You* could train such nurses. Think how well you have done with those you selected for the nursing home."

Florence shook her head. "I searched high and low for good, clean women like my own dear Nanny Gale at the institution. And you know how difficult it was to persuade any of them to come to us." She sighed. "No. Student nurses should be young women. From the farms and villages, perhaps — and you know what their people would say about that! And even if I could get them, where and how would I train them? Certainly the institution cannot provide money for such a project."

After Liz Herbert left, Florence paced her Harley Street sitting room, deep in thought.

If only there were some way to prove quickly what trained women could do to help suffering, sick persons! How much it would mean to the sufferers, and to the women themselves! It would not be an easy life, but it would be a satisfying, *useful* one. And it would add another honorable occupation for women who must earn their living, as well as those like herself, who were not content with only social and family duties.

Something *had* to be done. And then suddenly she thought of what *could* be done.

The "Call" Is Clear

FLORENCE sought out Dr. Bowman. He was the surgeon for the institution, and one of the best-known medical men of his day. She told him exactly what she wanted — an opportunity to train nurses on a large scale.

Dr. Bowman was quite familiar with the way Miss Nightingale managed to get what she wanted. His eyes twinkled. "And of course," he said, "knowing that I hold a senior appointment on the staff of King's College Hospital, you want me to use my influence to make such training possible."

Miss Nightingale did not even blush. "Yes," she said. "Since King's College Hospital is being rebuilt and reorganized, why not have the new professional nurse come from there?"

"Why not, indeed?" Dr. Bowman mused. If someone else had proposed such an idea, he would have said that person was mad. But Miss Nightingale was an extraordinary young woman. And judging by what she had accomplished at this nursing home. . . .

"As Superintendent of Nurses, I could select and thoroughly train the kind of women we need." Florence broke gently into his thoughts.

Dr. Bowman would not allow himself to be carried away by her enthusiasm. "Do you never consider the possibility of failure?" he asked her. "The type of woman you want in your training program will be hard to find. Young women from good homes would be discouraged by their families from entering nursing as it is now regarded."

"Given a chance, we could change the whole outlook on nursing," Florence told him confidently.

Dr. Bowman smiled. "Very well, Miss Nightingale. I shall see what can be done."

Several of the doctors at King's College hospital knew of Miss Nightingale's work at Harley Street. They were as impressed as Dr. Bowman with her talents.

"By all means, let us appoint her our Superintendent of Nurses," one of these gentlemen said at a Board of Directors meeting.

"She certainly cannot make things any worse," said another.

In August, while these discussions were going on, an epidemic of cholera struck London. And Florence's plans for training nurses had to be put aside during this terrible emergency.

Cholera, in 1854, was a fearful disease. It came suddenly, with high fever and terrible stomach pains. If a victim survived at all, he was weak and ill for days. But many more died than lived. The disease spread quickly through the slum districts where food and water were contaminated.

Wagon loads of frightened, hysterical patients were brought into the already overcrowded London hospitals. There was confusion everywhere. Many of the nurses caught the disease — many died of it. Others, terrified of infection, ran away.

Florence volunteered to superintend the nursing at Middlesex Hospital, but she ended up working harder than any of the ward nurses. From the Friday afternoon, when she reported at the hospital, till Sunday, no one saw her off her feet. She undressed, bathed, and treated the terror-stricken and pain-racked patients, comforting them as best she could. It did not matter to her whether they were wives and mothers from the poorest section of town, or wretched women of the streets. Each received the same gentle handling, tender care, and attention.

When the worst of the epidemic was over, Florence went to Lea Hurst to rest. There, a tearful Mrs. Nightingale told a house guest, "I do not understand Flo and her terrible work at all. We only wanted her to have every advantage — a good and comfortable life. We are ducks who have hatched a wild swan."

But it was no swan that they had hatched. As a famous writer put it years later, it was an eagle. And Florence Nightingale's courage and determination were soon to be known throughout the world.

Nightmare at Scutari

MEANWHILE, three thousand miles from London, events were happening that would affect the whole British Empire. They would also change Florence Nightingale's life forever.

Throughout the 1800's, England was a leading sea power in the world, and the British people depended on a vast world trade for their national wealth. To maintain its sea power, England had, for years, controlled the important entrance to the Mediterranean, as well as the eastern passage from the Mediterranean into the Black Sea — with the best navy in the world. But now England's power was threatened by Russia, whose Czar was determined to get control of the passageway from the Black Sea into the Mediterranean. If the Czar's navy could accomplish this, Russia could become a first-class naval power, and a real threat to French and English trade.

Therefore, when Russians began to move into Turkish towns that lay on the shores of the Black Sea, England

and France declared war. They planned to help Turkey win back these towns, and they also planned to destroy the new Russian naval base at Sevastopol, on the Crimean Peninsula of the Black Sea.

To the British people, three thousand miles from the Crimea, it seemed an easy thing to do, to defeat the Russians. After all, hadn't their army defeated the mighty Napoleon at Waterloo? But that was back in 1815, nearly forty years ago. Now, in 1854, the British army was no longer prepared for a full-scale war. Guns and equipment were old and out of date. Besides, fighting a war so far away required time and careful planning. National pride, however, would admit of no such thing. Some of the wiser heads in government realized the dangers. Even Queen Victoria and Prince Albert doubted the wisdom of this war. Nevertheless, patriotism prevailed. Men were drafted, equipment and supplies were hastily assembled, and the troops were gaily cheered as they sailed away, their bright uniforms blazing in the sun.

Pleasant weeks passed aboard the troop ships as they sailed along the coasts of France, Portugal, and Spain, and through the Strait of Gibraltar into the Mediterranean. More weeks passed, as the troop ships steamed past southern Italy and Greece. On they went through the Aegean Sea, through the Dardanelles, into the blue Sea of Marmara, through the Bosporus Strait, and on into the Black Sea. Men who had never been far from home were charmed by the sights and sounds of the pic-

RUSSIA

ROMANIA

BULGARIA

CRIMEA

Sea of Azov

Varna

Black Sea

Balaclava
Sevastopol

Constantinople

Scutari

Bosporus

Sea of Marmara

Dardanelles

TURKEY

0   200

Aegean Sea

0   20

CRIMEA

Mediterranean
Sea

Calamita
Bay

Alma R.

Katcha R.

Sevastopol

Duvankoi R.

Balaclava

Black Sea

•••• *ROUTE OF BRITISH ARMY*

turesque ports, where their ships put in for coal, water, and provisions.

An army base was set up in Scutari. This was a Turkish village on the Asian side of the Bosporus Strait. It lay directly across from Constantinople (now called Istanbul). Here the Turkish government had turned over to its British ally a huge old artillery barracks, and the General Hospital that went with it.

Some of the British soldiers were left at Scutari. Most of the army sailed on to Varna, a city on the Black Sea, in Bulgaria. From Varna they were supposed to make a swift and deadly thrust at Sevastopol, the Russian's naval base in the Crimea.

But when the transport ships arrived to move the army from Varna to the Crimea, there were not enough ships to take *both* men and equipment across the Black Sea. A fateful decision was quickly made, one that was to have disastrous consequences. It was decided to leave behind the general and medical supplies which always went with the army. Instead, only men, ammunition, and cavalry horses were jammed aboard the ships.

On the 14th of September, thirty thousand men landed at a cove, well-named Calamita Bay, thirty miles north of Sevastopol.

The staff surgeon was horrified. "They have sent out an army without any kind of hospital supplies," he exclaimed. "There are no litters or carts or pack animals. There is nothing to work with — when the time comes."

The time came a few days later. Dreaded cholera, the

black plague, broke out and spread rapidly. Without supplies, nothing could be done for the men. Over a thousand of the ill were shipped back to Scutari.

Six days later, the British and the French fought the Russians at the Battle of Alma — and won! Needless to say, the French army was better organized and equipped. For the British, it was a victory of sheer gallantry and courage. Both allied armies, fighting on foreign soil, had faced a withering fire from the Russian artillery.

Back in England, the people were overjoyed at the news of victory. Then the shocking casualty lists began to come in.

But even then the people at home had no idea of the real horror their soldiers were facing. They didn't know that the wounded were worse off than the dead. That because the supplies had been left in Varna, there were no bandages, no splints for broken, shattered bones, no anesthetics, no medicines. Soldiers lay on bare ground, or on dirty straw in farmyards, because bedding too had been left behind in Varna. Amputations were performed under the most filthy and brutal conditions. There were not even lamps or candles. At night surgeons had to work by moonlight.

But the horrors of the battlefield were soon equaled by the horrors at Scutari, when another thousand men with cholera were shipped back to the General Hospital there. It took from eight days to three weeks for these deathly sick men to reach Scutari. And when they did, their officers found that the first thousand cases filled every bed! The new cholera victims — those still alive — were placed on the floor anywhere there was space.

And now the Senior Medical Officer, Dr. Menzies, was notified that hundreds of those wounded at Alma would be arriving shortly! There was only one thing to do. The deserted old barracks must somehow be converted into a military hospital at once.

But how? The old barracks was enormous and filthy. How to get it cleaned? Where to get equipment? Dr. Menzies was still wrestling with this problem when the wounded began to arrive. They came in terrible condition. Ships meant to carry two hundred and fifty patients were crammed with more than twelve hundred. Soldiers with every kind of wound were thrown together, and all the way to Scutari they were tossed about cruelly by the rough seas.

When they arrived after the wrenching voyage, there were no beds to receive them — or nurses to care for them. They lay on the floor of the Barracks "Hospital," wrapped in blankets soaked with their blood. There was no food for them — because there was no hospital kitchen. There was no water — no one to carry it and nothing to carry it *in*. The doctors did what they could to save lives, working under these terrible conditions.

The British people might never have known about the nightmare horrors at Scutari if a war correspondent had not happened to be on the scene.

This man was William Howard Russell, of the London

Times — and he was the very first newspaper man to report from a battlefront.

The officers took no notice of him, but Russell noticed everything. And the reports he sent back to London, to the *Times,* were filled with fury and disgust.

His dispatches were published on October 9, 12, and 13 — and a whole nation reeled in shock.

"It is with feelings of surprise and anger," Russell wrote, "that the public will learn that no sufficient preparations have been made for the care of the wounded. Not only are there not sufficient surgeons . . . there is not even linen to make bandages. . . .

"There is no preparation for the commonest surgical operations! Not only are the men kept, in some cases, for a week without the hand of a medical man coming near their wounds, but now it is found that the commonest appliances of sick ward are wanting, and that the men must die through the medical staff of the British Army having forgotten that old rags are necessary for the dressing of wounds. . . ."

A bomb bursting on Buckingham Palace could not have stunned the British people more. Before they could recover from this blast, Russell sent another:

"The manner in which the sick and wounded are treated is worthy of savages. . . . There are no dressers or nurses to carry out surgeons' directions, and to attend on the sick between visits. Here the French are greatly our superiors. Their medical arrangements are extremely good, their surgeons more numerous, and they have also the help of the Sisters of Charity. . . . These devoted women are excellent nurses. . . ."

This last stung the public into even greater fury against the government. Indignant readers wrote to the *Times*. On October 14, a letter asked:

"Why have *we* no Sisters of Charity? There are numbers of able-bodied and tenderhearted English women who would joyfully go out to devote themselves to nursing the sick and wounded, if they could be organized for that purpose, and placed under proper protection."

While some asked questions, or wept, or seethed with rage, or wrung their hands helplessly, one English woman, Florence Nightingale, took direct action. On Saturday, October 14, five days after the first dispatch appeared in the *Times*, she wrote Liz Herbert:

". . . A small private expedition of nurses has been organized for Scutari and I have been asked to command it." She would pay her own expenses and those of one nurse, she told Liz. A contribution of two hundred pounds had been given for the expenses of three other nurses. These nurses would pay for their own lodgings and food and would be no expense whatever to the country. Florence had already seen Dr. Andrew Smith of the Army Medical Board, and he had given them authority to go.

"I do not mean that I believe the *Times* entirely," Florence added tactfully. After all, Sidney Herbert was now Secretary of War, and the target of many of the complaints, "but I do believe we may be of use to the poor wounded. . . ."

Florence's letter to Mrs. Herbert crossed Sidney Herbert's letter to her, written on Sunday, October 15.

"You will have seen in the papers," he wrote, "that there is a great deficiency of nurses at the hospital at Scutari. The other deficiencies, namely of medical men, lint, sheets, etc., have been remedied ere this . . . as to medical stores, they have been sent out in profusion. . . .

"But the deficiency of female nurses is undoubted, none but male nurses having been admitted to military hospitals. . . . It would be impossible to carry about a large staff of female nurses with the army in the field. But at Scutari no military reason exists against their introduction. . . .

"I have received numbers of offers from ladies to go out, but they are ladies who have no conception of what a hospital is, nor of the nature of its duties.

"There is but one person in England that I know of who would be capable of organizing and superintending such a scheme. . . . Would you listen to the request to go and superintend the whole thing? . . ."

Sidney Herbert then assured her that she would have complete authority over the nurses and the fullest assistance from the medical staff. Also she would have unlimited power to draw on the government for whatever she thought necessary for the success of her mission. . . .

"Your personal qualities, your knowledge, and your power of administration, and your rank and position in society give you advantages in such a work which no other person possesses," he wrote. Then he added,

"If this succeeds, an enormous amount of good will be done now, and a prejudice will have been broken. . . . I know you will come to a wise decision. God grant it may be in accordance with my hopes!"

It was a miracle, an undreamed of opportunity to change forever the tradition-bound views of nursing in England, in the world! Florence had never hoped for anything as big as this. The letter trembled in her hands as she read and reread it.

But before she had time to reply, Sidney Herbert had read Florence's letter and was on his way to her.

"There is more to this mission than relieving the sufferings of our soldiers," he told her as Florence led him into her sitting room. "The whole nation will be watching you. Bringing female nurses into an army hospital could be a calamity."

"Or a great victory," Florence said, her eyes fixed steadily on his.

"Yes," Mr. Herbert agreed. "If the nurses perform their duties well . . . If they prove that they are reliable, *no one will ever look down upon nurses again.*"

Florence glowed to hear him say it. To raise nursing to the level of a respected profession for women had been her dream for so long.

"It will not be easy to select the nurses you'll want to take with you," Sidney Herbert continued. "No one knows this better than you. I believe you should engage a group of forty!"

Florence gasped. "Forty! I doubt I shall be able to control more than twenty."

The Secretary of War smiled. "If you were anyone else, I would have my doubts too."

When Sidney Herbert left, Florence sat alone in her room for some time. Ever since that long day when she was seventeen and had heard the "Voice," she had known that someday she would be called to some very special mission. And now it had happened. God's purpose for her was clear at last.

But dreaming had long since given way to practicality, and Florence turned her attention to the immediate need. *Forty* nurses! Wherever was she to find them?

The Eagle Takes Wing

Everything moved swiftly now. Four days later, on Thursday, October 19, Florence was notified of her official appointment by the government as "Superintendent of the Female Nursing Establishment of the English General Hospitals in Turkey."

At once the whole country buzzed with excitement. Never before had a woman been so honored. Florence's family was as surprised as everyone else. But this time there were no hysterics. Suddenly Mrs. Nightingale and Parthe were enormously proud of their Flo. They hurried to see her in London.

Parthe now wrote a favorite cousin that: "It is a great and noble work . . . and one cannot but believe she was intended for it. None of her previous life has been wasted . . . her experience . . . the gathered stores of so many years . . ."

With her authority assured, Florence determined to waste no time in getting to Scutari. She set Saturday, October 21, as her sailing date. Her good friends,

Selina and Charles Bracebridge, had already volunteered to go with her and help her in every way they could. And Florence was pleasantly surprised and touched when her Harley Street matron, Mrs. Clarke, insisted that *she* was going too.

Three days to sailing! There was no time to lose. Charles Bracebridge took charge of the finances of the expedition and rushed about London making arrangements for the journey.

Sidney Herbert offered his London house as headquarters for the expedition. There a group of ladies, including Selina Bracebridge, Lady Canning, and Mary Stanley prepared to receive the women who applied as nurses. In high-sounding phrases, many English women had expressed their readiness to go and nurse their soldiers. But now only those of the humblest class showed up. And not many of them, either.

Florence Nightingale was able to select only fourteen elderly women who had had hospital experience. No young women were accepted, for the camp at Scutari was not a place for them. Florence had decided on plain uniforms — uniforms that would identify the women as nurses and serve as their protection among the rough soldiers. Moreover, each nurse was required to sign a pledge of absolute obedience to Miss Nightingale's orders.

The uniforms, warm and practical, consisted of a gray tweed dress and a gray worsted jacket. Across the front, each nurse would wear a band, embroidered in red with the words *Scutari Hospital*. A plain white cap, a bonnet, and a short woolen cloak completed the costume. Small white collars, and large white aprons would be worn on duty in and around the hospital.

Florence completed her nursing staff by enlisting twenty-four nuns and sisters from religious orders. She selected them "with a view to fitness and without any reference to religious creed." These nuns and sisters would wear the habit of their order rather than the uniform.

It scarcely seemed possible, but with Florence in charge it was, that by October 21, 1854, Miss Nightingale and her "Birds" — as the newspapers nicknamed her little band — were ready to leave.

As a last duty, Miss Nightingale called again on Dr. Andrew Smith, of the Army Medical Board, for possible advice. The doctor was in excellent humor. No doubt, he told Miss Nightingale, they would be a great comfort to the men. The ladies' finer instincts would discover such things as spots on a sheet — which male orderlies might overlook. And of course they could always give a nice soothing drink to the poor fellows who seemed uncomfortable.

Miss Nightingale managed to control herself. She said she was thinking of taking some needed supplies with her. The doctor laughingly assured her there was ample quantity of *everything* in Scutari — "a positive profusion of medical comforts."

After listening to him, Florence Nightingale decided to follow her own instincts — and added a few more items to her already lengthy list of supplies to take.

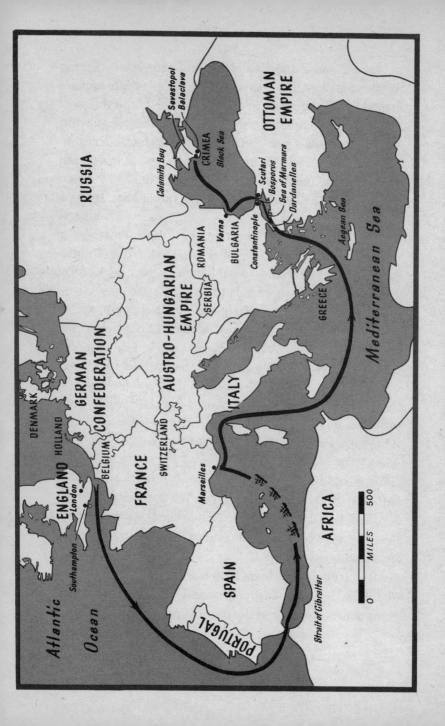

However, she took few personal possessions. Among these was a small black pocket notebook in which she had tucked three letters.

One of these was from her mother — the kind of letter she had hoped for, but never received till now. At long last Mrs. Nightingale blessed her daughter and her work. Another letter was from Bishop Manning, whose aid Florence had sought in enlisting the Catholic sisters as nurses. The third letter was from Richard Monckton Milnes.

"My Dear Friend," he wrote, "I hear you are going to the East. I am happy it is so for the good you will do there, and hope you may find some satisfaction in it yourself. . . . You can undertake *that*, when you could not undertake me. God bless you, dear friend, wherever you go."

On October 21, 1854, Florence Nightingale and her group of nurses left London. They crossed the English Channel to Boulogne, in France, where they were greeted enthusiastically by — among others — some French fisherwives. They knew who Florence was and where she was going — and many of them had sons, husbands, and brothers in the war.

The group continued on to Paris, and then to Marseilles, where they were to board a ship for Scutari. Florence spent several days in Marseilles purchasing large quantities of supplies. And when Florence and her "Birds" went aboard the mail boat, *Vectis,* on October 27, a mound of bales and boxes sailed with them.

The *Vectis* was a clumsy old paddle-wheeler, and on

the second day out she ran into a fierce storm. Florence was not a good sailor and had to take to her bed. The ship rolled, pitched, and shuddered as the seas pounded her. Parts of the ship, the steward's cabin, and the ship's galley, were washed away, but fortunately none of the crew or passengers was lost.

Somehow the wretched ship survived the raging weather, and on Saturday, November 4, she sailed up the Bosporus and dropped anchor.

This harbor was known as the Golden Horn, and the city of Constantinople curled around it on one side. The houses on the hills, the spires and minarets above the rounded domes of the Turkish mosques looked like a smudged watercolor in the drenching rain. Florence, who had managed to stagger up on deck, gazed at the scene briefly then turned to look at the opposite shore.

There sprawled the village of Scutari, with the huge, square Barracks Hospital set on a hill above it. Each side of the building was a quarter of a mile long, with a massive tower at each of the four corners.

The nurses and nuns lined the railing. Impulsively, one of them exclaimed, "Oh Miss Nightingale, when we land, don't let there be any delays! Let us get straight to nursing the poor fellows!"

Florence stared at the enormous building and shook her head. "More likely the strongest will be wanted at the wash tub." She sensed the disappointment around her, and her hands tightened on the ship's rail. Her nurses must be made to realize that there was nothing romantic about the work they had come to do. It would be hard and bitter and heartbreaking. Only the strongest in spirit would stand up to it. She turned abruptly and went back to her cabin.

Soon the British Ambassador at Constantinople, Lord Stratford, sent the Secretary of the Embassy to see Miss Nightingale.

The secretary delivered a flowery welcome from the ambassador, then informed her that she and her nurses were to go to Scutari at once. The Battle of Balaclava had been fought on October 25, and the wounded were expected to arrive soon.

Then brightly painted gondolalike boats — called caïques — appeared at the side of the *Vectis*. Miss Nightingale and her nurses, with their carpet bags and umbrellas, were lowered into them. As the Turkish boatmen rowed them across the white-capped bay, the caïques bobbed and dipped alarmingly. The rain had stopped and the shore could be seen more clearly, with its rickety dock and the steep slopes above it. There was no sign of a paved road and, as Flo was helped to the dock, she wondered about the wounded. How on earth did they get them up to the hospital?

Florence and Mr. and Mrs. Bracebridge led the procession toward the huge main entrance of the hospital. Their messenger-interpreter followed, and the nurses trailed behind. The Barracks Hospital, looming above them, looked so forbidding that Selina Bracebridge reached out and gripped Flo's hand. Everything looked worse, the closer they got. Garbage and litter were everywhere, and in the building dozens of broken windows gaped to the winds.

Perhaps it was not so bad inside, Florence told herself. After all, Mr. Herbert and Dr. Smith had assured her that all necessities had been sent here.

Dr. Menzies, the Senior Medical Officer, and Major Sillery, the Military Commandant, met them at the gate. The men said the proper words of greeting. They asked polite questions about their journey. But Florence could find no trace of genuine welcome in either man. Well, she had not expected to be received with open arms. She and her nurses would have to prove themselves.

Major Sillery appeared nervous. "Of course you'll want to get settled," he said. "We have assigned you the North West Tower. It has a number of rooms and you will have more privacy there. If you will follow me. . . ."

The women picked their way through the muddy, littered square enclosed by the barracks. One side of the huge building had been gutted by fire and stood unused.

As the officers led the way, Dr. Menzies was silent, controlling his anger. The last thing he wanted in this hospital was a pack of women to pamper the soldiers. As for this youngish society lady — at best she might turn out to be a well-bred nuisance. At worst, she might well be a government spy. And Dr. Menzies had something to fear on that account.

He remembered his interview with the Ambassador at Constantinople, Lord Stratford. The ambassador had received a letter from the government questioning the conditions at the Barracks Hospital. The ambassador had told Dr. Menzies that if there were shortages, as reported, there were also large sums of public money available for anything needed. After those dreadful articles by that man Russell, donations had poured in to the government. The *Times* also had a special fund to be used for anything at all that was needed.

Dr. Menzies was horrified. His superior officer, Dr. Hall, had already sent an "all's well" report to England. If he consented now to use public funds, Dr. Menzies would be admitting that everything had been bungled. Instead he told the ambassador that all present needs were taken care of. As for the future, there were the supplies at Varna. Nothing was needed. Nothing.

The ambassador readily accepted Dr. Menzie's assurances and chose to ignore the trouble-making reporter. He never bothered to make a personal inspection, nor did he send anyone from his staff to do so. Instead he wrote Mr. Herbert that everything was fine, and there was a "profusion of supplies."

Now here was Miss Nightingale — an intimate friend of the Minister of War! Just what was she after? Much as he'd like to send her packing at this very moment, Dr. Menzies didn't dare. She had powerful friends at home.

The group climbed a steep flight of steps. Major Sillery threw open the door leading into the tower, "Six rooms," he said. "All yours."

The rooms were dark, damp, and filthy. Florence

could see no furniture, except for a few chairs. There were no tables, no beds. No stoves to cook on or give off heat. Around the walls of some of the rooms ran raised wooden platforms — but there was no bedding visible anywhere. The more Flo looked, the worse it all appeared — and, she suspected, *not* by accident.

Major Sillery coughed apologetically. "You must understand that we can provide little in the way of accommodations, Miss Nightingale. Our first concern is for our men."

Florence smiled. "But that is as it should be," she said evenly.

The Major's color heightened. He appealed to Dr. Menzies. "The Doctor will tell you that we are all terribly crowded here."

"Yes, yes," agreed the Doctor. "We are overcrowded already and more casualties are expected tomorrow."

Major Sillery nodded vigorously. "So you see, we have little room to spare."

"This will do very well." Miss Nightingale inclined her small, elegant head. "Thank you."

The Doctor and the Major excused themselves. The door closed behind them — and Selina exploded.

"Florence, this will never do! Never! Six rooms for more than forty people!"

Flo looked around. "One of these 'rooms' is a store room. We'll make a kitchen of it." She was already planning ahead. "And one a closet — I'd say ten feet square. The sixth room must be upstairs — "

"We can't possibly manage in this space," Selina insisted. "What can they be thinking?"

"They can be thinking that if we are uncomfortable enough we will go home on the next boat. That is exactly what they want. It is not what I intend to do," Flo answered calmly.

Charles Bracebridge stomped about furiously. "But this is disgraceful. I'll speak with the Major myself."

Flo stopped him. "I think it would not do any good. He must do what he is told — and Dr. Menzies' mind is clearly made up about us."

Tired and disappointed, the nurses began to murmur among themselves.

Florence took charge at once. "For the time being at least, we will have to make the best of things," she told them. "Now then, we'll put fourteen nurses in this large room and ten in the next. Selina, you and I will take the closet. Charles and our messenger can have the small room." The nuns were assigned the sixth room upstairs, and obediently they picked up their carpet bags and trudged up the stairs. A moment later shrieks were heard, and the eight nuns clattered down the stairs.

Florence's Battle at Scutari

PALE AND SHAKEN, one of the nuns cried, "Miss Nightingale, the room upstairs is occupied —"

Flo frowned. "Surely, Sister, if you explained who you were —"

The nun shook her head. "The man is dead. He looks like a Russian general."

"Really, this is too much," Charles Bracebridge exclaimed. He stormed out of their quarters, followed by the interpreter. They came back with two Turkish orderlies who removed the body.

If Miss Nightingale wondered how and why a dead general — a prisoner of war — had just happened to be overlooked in a tower assigned to her, she said nothing.

"What we all need," said Selina, "is a nice, hot cup of tea."

It sounded so much like home that Flo laughed and it broke the tension. She felt her strength returning. "I'll go down to the kitchen and see what can be found. Why don't you all start to unpack?" she suggested.

"We'll need brooms and scrubbing brushes," said Sister Margaret.

"I don't seem to be able to find the bedding anywhere," said Mrs. Roberts, one of the nurses.

Florence set off with a long list of the things they needed. An hour later she returned with forty tin basins and a large pot of milkless tea. It was all she could find. They drank it huddled together, while Flo reported what she had seen.

"I'm afraid that nothing we read in the *Times* could have prepared us for the actual conditions here. There is no furniture and no equipment in this place. The men are lying out there on the bare floor, row upon row, shivering with cold. They have no shirts and no bedding. In one ward, an operation was being performed before the eyes of all the other wounded men. They did not even have an operating table."

The nurses were shocked into silence.

"The kitchen is impossible," Florence continued. "They seem to use thirteen huge Turkish copper pots to cook everything — for all those men. There are no baking ovens, no proper utensils. And there seems to be only the one kitchen."

"Thank goodness you thought to bring some supplies and utensils for us," exclaimed Selina. "Our stores should come in off the *Vectis* in a day or so. But the poor men!"

Florence silenced her friend with a gesture. Such outbursts accomplished nothing. She had already resolved to waste no energy in futile anger, reproaches, or vain hopes. Every ounce of strength she had would be used to forward the success of her mission.

"For the present," she continued calmly, "the tin basins you are holding are going to have to do triple duty. They'll be used for washing, eating, and drinking tea."

The nurses stared at their basins, scarcely able to believe what they were hearing.

"Er . . . ah . . . Flo," Charles Bracebridge announced reluctantly. "There seems to be a shortage of water too. The young chap outside tells me there is a fountain in the corridor. We are to be rationed one pint each day."

"For everything?" Mrs. Clarke sounded scandalized.

"For washing and drinking and tea," Mr. Bracebridge said heavily.

That night they all went to bed in the dark, for they had been given neither lamps nor candles. Somehow they managed without bedding, lying on the hard wooden benches or the dirty floor.

"At least we are all well," one of the women spoke out of the darkness. And all the others knew that she was thinking of the much greater suffering of the wounded in the halls beyond.

Florence lay awake beside Selina Bracebridge, staring into the darkness of their stuffy closet. All the knowledge she had acquired about nursing would be needed now. But would Dr. Menzies and Major Sillery allow her to use her knowledge?

"*Flo!*" Selina's urgent tone startled her.

"What's wrong?" Florence raised herself and peered at her friend.

"Do you hear what I hear?"

Both women sat silently, listening. There was the

sound of tiny, scurrying feet and high-pitched, eerie squeaks.

Flo sighed. They might have expected this too. "Rats, Selina, rats! We'll have to do what we can in the morning. Try to get some sleep now."

"*Sleep!*" echoed Selina. "Oh, Flo!"

Somehow they did sleep. In the morning they lined up at the fountain to get their ration of water. When they returned to their quarters, they found several pails of food that had been left for them in the large central room of the Tower.

Mrs. Clarke bent over to inspect it and pronounced it, "Slop!" However, everyone was so hungry that they closed their eyes, ignored the smell, and ate what they could.

By this time Florence had decided to station twenty-eight nurses for duty in the Barracks Hospital, and ten in the General Hospital that stood a quarter of a mile away. But the one rule she must abide by at all costs was that *no nurse was to enter a ward without the request of the doctor in charge.* Her appointment plainly stated that she was to work under the orders and direction of the Chief Army Medical Officer — Dr. Menzies. She waited all that day, but no orders came from Dr. Menzies.

"Perhaps that is because it is Sunday," one of the disappointed nurses remarked.

Florence exchanged a swift glance with Charles Bracebridge and immediately suggested that they go to the Barrack chapel to hear the sermon. If the doctors did not choose to use her nurses, she would have to keep them occupied in other ways.

Happily, their supplies from the *Vectis* began to arrive. Florence had the boxes opened and set some of her nurses to sorting the old linen that would be used for soft dressings. Provisions had to be counted, sorted, and listed. Florence intended to keep track of every item that came or went to the Tower. Too many supplies intended for the soldiers had vanished without a trace. She would be able to account for every item, and for every penny spent from the money entrusted to her.

As she worked among her nurses, Flo kept her ears tuned for sounds of unusual movement outside their Tower. The wounded from the disastrous Battle of Balaclava were expected to arrive today. Surely then she and her nurses would be called.

These would be the brave survivors of one of the most terrible battles of the Crimean War. The gallant light-cavalry brigade had been almost wiped out there. They had followed confused orders and charged straight into a massed Russian cannon. Whatever "victory" was won had come through the sheer courage of the common soldiers. These were the men Florence now hoped to nurse — if the doctors would set aside their prejudices against women in army hospitals. So far, she had received none of the cooperation promised to her back in England.

"Flo." Charles Bracebridge appeared at her side. "They're landing the poor fellows now. It's horrible."

After days on a rough sea, the wounded were lowered from the hospital ship into boats. For most of the men this was torture. They were bumped and tossed over to the dock where careless Turkish orderlies hauled them onto stretchers. Their pitiful cries went unheeded. Inside the Barracks Hospital, where they had hoped for some comfort, they were dumped heedlessly on the bare floor. There were so many that most were left untended. It was like the *Times* account all over again.

From the windows of their quarters, the nurses watched the horrible scenes on the slopes. Florence hurried to Dr. Menzies and offered the services of her nurses.

"We could bathe the wounded and bring them water," she said. "Some of us would be willing to help carry stretchers. The men are suffering so."

Dr. Menzies eyed her coldly. "The British soldier is not a namby-pamby school boy, Miss Nightingale. You do not give the men credit for their extraordinary physical courage. Your nurses," he added, "would only embarrass them. They would be in the way."

Without another word, Florence returned to her quarters. She would not offer to send her nurses into the wards again. If she insisted, Dr. Menzies would consider it a threat to his authority. He might never forgive her. Then she and her nurses could give up all hope of becoming a useful part of the hospital. They would have to wait — no matter how difficult that waiting was — until they were *asked* to help in the wards.

The nurses did not understand this. They knew only

that they had come to help the British soldiers. They wanted to rush outside and do whatever they could for the suffering soldiers. When Florence refused to permit this, they became angry.

"It's inhuman, that's what it is," one of them muttered. "How can we stand by and watch them die without doing anything?"

For a moment Florence thought she had lost control and they would disobey her orders. If that happened, all that she hoped to accomplish would be defeated then and there.

She stood before them, commanding them, willing them to obey her. She did not raise her voice and her manner remained calm. "You must understand," she told them, "that we are something entirely new to the British Army. We must not behave like undisciplined hysterical females. If we do, the authorities will send us home in disgrace. We *can* help the wounded men — even here, in our Tower."

For the next several days she kept them rolling bandages, folding soft dressings, making stump-rests for the amputees, and slings for broken legs and arms. Mrs. Bracebridge and Mrs. Clarke sorted provisions and stacked them in the store room. Mr. Bracebridge and the interpreter went down to the village and rounded up odd pieces of furniture and bedding for the Tower.

Meanwhile, Florence continued her inspection of the hospital. Somehow she must find a way for her nurses to be useful outside the Tower. It must be a way that would meet with Dr. Menzie's approval.

Down in the hospital kitchen she found an attendant on duty who was willing to talk. Stepping back from a huge steaming kettle, he wiped his damp forehead with a grubby rag.

"I tell you, Miss, it's a great burden this job. We prepare three different kinds of meals here, you know. There's full rations — that is the soldiers' regular diet." He turned to a table, picked up some chunks of meat tied together with a piece of torn uniform and dropped them into the copper kettle. Several other chunks were held together with red string. These he dropped in also.

Florence tried to keep the horror from showing in her face. She made her voice even as she said, "May I ask why the meat is tied up in that way?"

The man looked surprised at her ignorance. "Why, Miss, that's for telling what belongs to what orderly. How else would we know unless the meat was tied up different?"

When he saw that Miss Nightingale still did not understand, he went on. "Look here, each orderly takes care of so many soldiers. He gets their rations himself with a signed paper from the doctor. We cook it for them here all together. But how are we to know who gets what amount of meat? So we mark it like this, with rope or a nail or a hook for the joints. Then each orderly claims what is his."

Florence watched as he began to ladle a stew — if it could be called that — from another copper pot into pails lined up beside it.

"Some men get full rations and some get only half.

But a lot of 'em are on spoon diet now, poor chaps. There's lots of stomach ailments here. It's up to the orderly to give the food out according to doctor's instructions. We do everything by the book here, Miss. No signed paper, no food," he finished proudly.

The smoke from the green wood fires made her eyes smart, but Florence continued her questions.

"What about extras like milk pudding or jelly? Surely those on liquid diet need more than — " she stared at the muddy water in which the meat had cooked, "than this soup?"

The man shrugged. "Oh, Miss, we've no place to make extras even if we could get them."

Florence thanked him for explaining things to her and went immediately to find Dr. Menzies. It was no wonder the wounded often died of illnesses other than their wounds. The terrible food and filthy conditions would make healthy men sick.

She found Dr. Menzies at last, busy in one of the wards. Whatever might be said about him, he was a tireless doctor. He worked as quickly and efficiently as possible, but there were always more men arriving than he could handle. When Florence reached him, he looked exhausted, too exhausted to argue.

She plunged right in. "Dr. Menzies, I know you do not approve of having my female nurses working in the wards. But we could help by supervising the cooking of special diets for the men. Your kitchen is overburdened and we would not interfere there, of course. We will make our own arrangements. Won't you let us provide the men with arrowroot and port wine? At least these will help to lessen their hunger pangs. Many have not eaten properly in weeks — " She paused and wondered if she had gone too far.

A frown began to gather on Dr. Menzies' forehead, and Florence said quickly, "We will observe all the usual rules and will never act without signed orders from the doctors. Please let us help."

Dr. Menzies gazed at Florence wearily. There was so much to do . . . so many men to attend to. Now *she* was bothering him again. Perhaps if he let her fuss with diets it would keep her so busy she would leave him alone.

"Very well!" he snapped. "See to it, if you like. But mind you," he warned, "the proper forms must be filled out. You are to do nothing without permission."

Florence nodded and sped away. The army was simply mad about proper procedures and correct forms. It was bogged down with paper work, signing and countersigning everything. She would go right along with the rules, now that she had a foothold. Here was something her nurses could do for the men directly.

The store room in the nurses' quarters soon became an "extra diet" kitchen, with Mrs. Clarke presiding over its precious stores. Florence had bought portable stoves as well as quantities of arrowroot powder. Mixed with boiling water this swelled into a kind of starchy jelly, easily digested by the sick. Wine served to warm and brace the weakened men. Beef extracts, rice, and sago-thickened puddings were useful in restoring a little of their strength.

So it was that the survivors of Balaclava were fed proper, soft, invalid foods from clean pails carried by Florence Nightingale's nurses. But the nurses were instructed to do nothing, *absolutely nothing* else.

With the Tower kitchen running smoothly, Florence began to plan another one. At this time there were nearly two thousand sick and wounded in the Barracks Hospital wards. Florence thought of putting a second kitchen at the opposite end of the building.

On Thursday, November 9, as she hurried past the wards to inspect the site, she came upon Dr. Menzies addressing a group from his medical staff.

"Half an hour!" exclaimed one of the doctors in response to something the Chief said. "How can we possibly get ready to receive five hundred men on a half-hour's notice!"

Dr. Menzies' shoulders sagged. His face was ashen. "I don't know. Some oversight in notifying us. . . . These are the poor devils from Inkerman. . . ."

Florence's heart lurched. The dreadful battle of Inkerman had been fought on November 5, and now five hundred of the wounded were coming when there was scarcely enough room for the men already here!

"We must do what we can," Dr. Menzies was saying. "Round up everybody who can help. We must use every pair of hands we can find. *Miss Nightingale!*" he roared suddenly. "Where are your nurses?"

The other doctors turned to her. Their prejudices were suddenly forgotten. Miss Nightingale represented forty pairs of hands! At a time as desperate as this, desperate measures must be taken — even if it meant using civilian females as nurses in a British Army Hospital!

In the face of such an overwhelming emergency, a lesser spirit would have collapsed. Not Florence. Even as she sped back to the Tower to alert her people, she was already putting first things first.

The men must be bedded somewhere. Since there was little room left in the wards, the great cold halls would have to be used. There were no beds — no mattresses. But there was a stable of cavalry horses in the barracks and tons of straw for them.

Flo sent Charles Bracebridge and the interpreter to round up some orderlies and find any kind of material that could be stitched up into great sacks. Then she set her nurses to stuffing the sacks with straw.

"Between one and nine o'clock we had the mattresses stuffed, sewn up, laid down — alas! only upon matting on the floor — the men washed and put to bed, and all their wounds dressed. . . ." she wrote a few days later to her good friend, Dr. Bowman, in England.

"We have now *four miles* of beds, and not eighteen inches apart. . . ."

But this was not the end of the flood of sick and wounded — only the beginning.

Supply Officer Extraordinary

"THE WOUNDED are now lying up to our very door," Florence wrote in a letter home. They lay crowded in the two corridors, between the nurses' Tower and the main gate, because the four wards were filled to capacity. "We are landing 540 more," she added.

Sick and wounded . . . sick and wounded. . . . They came in a never-ending stream. If so many had not died, the new arrivals would have had to lie outdoors. In the hospital they ran out of mattress bags and straw. The wounded were laid upon the bare floors, with their boots under their heads — if they had boots. They were wrapped in their blood-stiffened coats — if they were lucky enough to have coats.

Battles did not account for all these casualties and hardships. Much of this suffering was the result of official mistakes which went on all through the campaign.

The Russians still held their naval base, Sevastopol. The British Army, commanded by Lord Raglan, camped on the heights above the seaport, their supply camp seven miles below, at Balaclava.

The November Battle at Inkerman had been won by the British, but again with a terrible loss of men. Several grim facts became obvious. The Russians had no intention of surrendering. Their position was still strong, and it was clear at this point that no quick victory could be gained. The British troops were exhausted, winter was setting in — and the soldiers were not prepared for the bone-chilling cold.

When the troops were first landed on the peninsula in October, the heat had been stifling. The seven-mile march to the heights was so grueling that the officers ordered the men to abandon their packs along the way. These packs contained everything a soldier needed, yet no provision was made to bring these up to the campsite later.

Now, in November, the weather changed suddenly — and the men had only their mud-caked *summer* uniforms. There was no proper shelter for them. There were no warm blankets, no warm clothes — not even enough food. The Army could not withdraw from its position on the heights — nor could it get enough supplies brought up. The dirt roads had become rivers of mud.

The sanitary conditions became so bad that soon hundreds of soldiers were stricken with cholera.

Every bed in the army hospitals in the Crimea was filled. The men who did not die at the camp or down at the base were carried by ship to Scutari. Florence's nurses had more than enough to keep them busy now. And Florence, who was supposed to be their Lady Superintendent, and direct their activities, now worked in the wards. She also assisted at the operations and amputations. These were still usually performed without anesthesia, in the wards and corridors, in sight of all the other men.

Many men died of fevers and the wound infections that followed every operation. Antiseptic methods and sterile hospital conditions were still years away. It was a miracle that any one survived the surgery.

"Oh, you gentlemen of England," Florence wrote Dr. Bowman, "you can have little idea, from reading the newspapers, of the horror and misery (in a military hospital) of operating on these dying, exhausted men. A London hospital is a garden of flowers compared to this."

The work of Florence and her nurses did not pass unnoticed. One young doctor was especially impressed.

"I could use a hundred nurses like them," he told Florence. "No, two hundred. It's a blessing you've come at a time like this. We could never have managed."

To Florence, *his* words were a blessing. She knew Dr. McGrigor worked with no thought of sparing himself.

"You have been on your feet more than twenty-four hours," she reminded him gently.

"These men have been suffering longer than that. I can't stop now," and he added, with a weary smile, "You have not rested much yourself, Miss Nightingale."

That was true. But the hospital was filled and still more men kept arriving. How could she rest?

One day, as Florence passed through a ward, Sister Margaret Goodman hurried to her. "Miss Nightingale, some of the men who have just arrived refuse to let us help them. They say they are so filthy their own mothers wouldn't touch them. If only we could give them some clean clothes!"

But there were no clean clothes, no supplies, no fresh food. Bitterly, Flo thought of the ship from England, the *Prince,* that had steamed right past Scutari though it was loaded with desperately needed supplies for the hospital. It went on to the Crimea instead, to deliver ammunition. Now they would have to wait until the *Prince* returned. Until then . . .

Whenever she passed a window, Florence would look out at the Strait of Bosporus, hoping to catch sight of the ship. On Tuesday, November 14, she thought the Strait was unusually rough, and the tides remarkably high.

That night she and Selina were awakened by a strange, thrumming wind.

"What can it mean?" Selina asked.

Florence shook her head. "This area is subject to sudden shifts in weather. It can mean anything — but certainly a storm somewhere."

For a long time, she lay awake worrying about the men in the wards and corridors — and thinking of the many broken windows that had not yet been repaired. If only they had more blankets . . . But until the *Prince* returned, no one at the hospital seemed to know of any way to get the things needed by the men. When Florence asked Dr. Menzies, he referred her to Major Sillery. The Major in turn looked distressed, but said it was not his department. Therefore, it was not his responsibility, according to Army Regulations. He sent her to old Mr. Ward.

Mr. Ward, who was at least seventy, was called a purveyor. He was in charge of buying and distributing supplies. He was polite, but firm.

"According to regulations," he said, "the men are supposed to bring their packs with them to the hospital. In the packs they have a change of clothing, eating utensils, razors, combs, brushes, soap — all the things you are requiring of me now, Miss Nightingale."

"The men have no packs," Florence pointed out. "You know as well as I that they were *ordered* to abandon them in the field."

"Nevertheless," Mr. Ward insisted, "I have no signed orders to replace anything. So you see, I can do nothing."

Florence saw — only too well. Everyone in charge was so tied and bound in the red tape of regulations that no one dared make an independent move. Yet it was obvious to everyone that this was an emergency — that men were dying for want of necessities. Well, in a few days the *Prince* would be returning, and then there would be some relief to this impossible situation.

A few days later, Charles Bracebridge appeared before Florence with the terrible news. "The *Prince* and all the supplies have been lost," he told her.

Selina covered her face with her hands and wept.

Florence gazed out of the window while she fought for self-control. "How did it happen?" she asked at last.

"Remember the strange wind and the high tides on the 14th?" Charles said. "There was a hurricane — the worst they've seen in years on the peninsula. Not a tent is left standing. They say even horses were blown for miles. All the ships in Balaclava harbor have been sunk — including the *Prince*."

Dr. Menzies found it impossible to provide even the simplest necessities for his patients. The men themselves seemed to have given up hope, and the wards were strangely, heartbreakingly quiet. At this point, Florence Nightingale decided to take matters into her own hands.

She knew that a Mr. Macdonald had been sent out by the London *Times* to supervise the spending of all the money — the thousands of pounds — collected by his paper for the relief of the soldiers. She also knew that so far no one had bothered to accept what he had to offer. Florence asked Charles Bracebridge to arrange a meeting at once.

Mr. Macdonald had seen Florence in action in the wards. When Charles brought him to the nurses' Tower, Mr. Macdonald immediately put himself at Miss Nightingale's disposal.

"I felt sure that I could count on your cooperation," Florence told him. "I too have a large sum of money with me. Thirty thousand pounds, donated by people anxious to change this terrible situation. But the hospital officials say they must get their supplies from England. *Regulations,* you know," she added wryly. "I suggest that we can obtain what is necessary right here."

"No question about it!" Mr. Macdonald assured Flo. "I can get everything you need in Constantinople. It's one of the largest markets in the world. If you'll trust me to do the purchasing, I'll go to Constantinople this very morning."

Florence handed over the list she had ready. It was a long one. The first item was two hundred scrubbing brushes — and sack cloth for the cleaning of the hospital walls and floors. Then there were warm woolen clothing for the men, knives, forks, spoons, tin cups, towels, and soap.

Carefully Mr. Macdonald checked off Flo's lists for food, tables, trays, clocks, scissors for the trimming of the men's hair, fine-toothed combs, and a solution for destroying lice. She also wanted operating tables — so the patients would not be laid upon rickety boards set on trestles. And she ordered screens for the operating tables, so the poor fellows, waiting to be operated on, would not see the sufferings of their comrades. "The terrible impression puts such fear into their minds, it lessens their chances of survival," she told him.

When urgently needed supplies suddenly began to appear, the doctors stared in wonder. It did not take them long to discover where they came from. But so desperate was the situation that the doctors accepted everything and asked no questions. Soon Miss Nightingale became known as the unofficial purveyor — or Supply Officer — for anything needed. The words, "Go to Miss Nightingale" were as powerful a charm as "Open Sesame." She always managed to have or to find anything required — and with the least possible delay. However, she never allowed anything to be issued from her private stores without a signed request from the medical officers.

No food from her stores was ever given to any patient under any circumstances, without a specific order from the doctor in charge. This often angered the nurses. But Florence knew this was the proper course to take. *Nurses must always act under doctors' orders. Otherwise fatal errors might be made.* Florence had no intention of breaking any hospital rules.

Florence's first step, when a request came in, was to check with Mr. Ward. If he said the item was not in stock, she added it to her "shopping" list. Mr. Macdonald then fetched it from Constantinople.

Mr. Ward was heard to complain bitterly that Miss Nightingale never gave him enough *time* to get anything. She was always rushing off to get whatever was wanted on her own. But Florence was well aware that Mr. Ward's idea of *time* meant weeks or months — if ever.

Once, Florence received an order for warm shirts for the men at Balaclava. She knew that a shipment of 27,000 shirts had been sent from England — at her suggestion. They had arrived — but the purveyor said he could not unpack them until the Board of Survey inspected and released them. Florence promptly had similar shirts bought and shipped from Constantinople. Old Mr. Ward fumed in Scutari. After all, he complained, she could have had the government shirts in three weeks or so. The fact that the soldiers were lying half-naked and shivering, and needed the shirts immediately was beside the point. Mr. Ward insisted that Miss Nightingale had behaved in a most irregular and unmilitary manner.

The responsibility which Florence Nightingale had assumed increased the comings and goings in the nurses' Tower. Now orderlies with doctors' requests were always waiting at the door of her small office. A member of her staff checked each request to see that it was properly signed and countersigned before any supplies were given out.

Her staff called their quarters the Tower of Babel. At all hours everything seemed to be there — boxes, parcels, bundles of sheets, shirts, old linen and flannels, tubs of butter, sugar, bread, kettles, saucepans — besides the special diets which were being cooked and served.

Under Miss Nightingale's direction, and at her *insistence*, the wards were finally cleaned. Next she turned her attention to the washing of the men's clothes and bedding.

She rented a Turkish house nearby, and had hot-water boilers installed. Then she hired the soldiers' wives, who had come out from England with their men, to do the washing.

The two hospitals in Scutari were beginning to emerge from chaos into some sort of order. But both were still terribly overcrowded. Then early in December, the Commander-in-Chief of the Army, Lord Raglan, sent word that five hundred more patients were being shipped to Scutari!

The medical staff held a desperate council.

"We can't possibly cram another man into these wards or corridors," Dr. McGrigor said. "If only we had the use of the burned-out wing of this place! But I suppose there isn't any money to repair it. And no one would have the authority to order the construction."

Florence looked out across the open court at the fourth side of the huge square that formed the Barracks Hospital. This section of the hospital had been badly gutted by fire before the British arrived. But she knew there was space there for two large wards. And with the corridor between the wards, room for almost a thousand additional patients. The repairs would be costly — and the red tape almost endless. But it could be done.

"Our ambassador here, Lord Stratford, has all the

money and authority that's needed," Florence told Dr. McGrigor. Had not Sidney Herbert assured her again and again that Lord Stratford had been directed to spare no expense for the well-being of the British soldiers?

Dr. McGrigor laughed shortly. "The Ambassador? Miss Nightingale, you can't be serious. He lives in that palace of his in plain sight of this hospital. He knows full well the difficulties we've had. And he has not lifted a finger to help!"

"I shall ask him nevertheless," said Florence Nightingale.

An Unwelcome Addition

FLORENCE immediately sent a message to the Ambassador, stating the urgent situation at the Barracks Hospital. To everyone's surprise, 125 Turkish men were hired to build the wards in the burned-out section. But it was a short-lived triumph. After a few days the workers decided their pay was too low and they went on strike. Florence wrote to the Ambassador. The Ambassador said there was nothing he could do.

Once more Florence acted on her own. She went out and hired 200 men, on her own responsibility. Again she paid for the workers and the materials with private funds.

And so "the wards were ready to receive the 500 men from the ships *Ripon* and *Golden Fleece*," Florence reported to Sidney Herbert.

The soldiers were in the last stages of exhaustion — cold, weak, starved, and filthy. They were quickly washed, given clean clothes, and put into clean beds.

These beds were set on wooden stands, raised about a foot from the floor — and built at the direction of Miss Nightingale. No sooner were the men settled, than her nurses hurried in with warm food — arrowroot, ladled out of huge milk pails, containing generous portions of port wine. Florence had supplied all the utensils for this wing, since the purveyor could provide nothing. Her contribution included "knives, forks, spoons, cans, towels, etc.," she wrote Mr. Herbert.

After the hardships endured at Balaclava and aboard ship, the soldiers could scarcely believe their good fortune. One of them said, "We felt we were in heaven."

Now, the doctors — even Dr. Menzies — at Scutari had nothing but praise for Florence Nightingale. On the peninsula, however, some of the officers were resentful of her "high-handed" actions. Her boldness in the face of regulations shocked them. How dared she spend all that money without consulting anyone? Surely now the government would set her down.

Instead, Miss Nightingale received complete approval from the War Department. Moreover, every penny she spent was refunded to her. This demonstration of "the Nightingale power" greatly strengthened her position.

But Florence's primary concern was not with personal glory and power. Her real mission was still to prove the value of women as nurses. Her nurses were busy enough now, yet the quality of their work and their personal behavior often caused her anxiety.

Of her original group of thirty-eight, Florence had found sixteen women who were really dependable. Six were exceptional. Mrs. Roberts, from St. Thomas' Hospital in London, was "worth her weight in gold." Mrs.

Drake, from St. John's House, "was a treasure." And of course there was the Reverend Mother from Bermondsey and her nuns. They were Florence's faithful supporters. But among the others, one nurse had been sent home already for improper conduct . . . and there were two more who must be dismissed . . . and there was Mrs. Lawfield.

Florence had a keen sense of humor and was able to see the funny side of many situations. All her life it was this ability that helped her through bitter disappointments — and the Mrs. Lawfields of the world.

"I came out, Ma'am, prepared to submit to everything, to be put upon in every way. But there are some things, Ma'am, one can't submit to. . . ." Flo's lips twitched in amusement as she recalled that conversation with plump, elderly Mrs. Lawfield. "There is the *caps*, Ma'am, that suits one face and some that suits another. And if I'd known, Ma'am, about the *caps*, great as was my desire to come out to nurse at Scutari, I wouldn't have come, Ma'am."

Still, Mrs. Lawfield was turning into a truly able nurse. Faced with real emergencies, she had become resigned to her cap. Perhaps the other women would also turn into reliable nurses. But it was so hard to instil discipline — the strict obedience to orders — the need for personal conduct beyond reproach. . . .

Florence sighed. There was her sense of mission about nursing. And her responsibility to Sidney Herbert. If they failed, *he* would be blamed for sending women out to military hospitals.

And yet, Florence thought, she had every right to be satisfied with the way things were going. So much good had come of their being here. The lines of her mouth softened as she thought of the hundreds of men lying in the wards and corridors all around this tower. She was beginning to think of them as her "children." They were so brave. They bore the pain of their dreadful wounds, disease, and privations with such heroism, without complaints. And they were so touchingly grateful for every attention.

With a soft swish of her full black merino skirt, Florence settled herself at the small unpainted table in the room she shared with Selina Bracebridge. She adjusted the wick of the lamp and the light glowed on her earnest face. Her chestnut hair was almost hidden under her plain white cap. She tied a black kerchief over the cap and wrapped her wool shawl more tightly about her shoulders. It was so cold and damp in Scutari and they never had enough fuel. Florence hated the cold, but she would not allow herself to think about it. She dipped her quill pen into the ink bottle and prepared to write Sidney Herbert of their accomplishments thus far. "December 14, 1854 . . ."

Florence and Selina carried on a huge and necessary correspondence, and reserved the quiet hours of the night for the reading and writing of letters. "Do you realize, Selina," said Florence, "that we have already supplied the men with 2,000 shirts?"

Selina Bracebridge did not seem to hear. She was absorbed in a letter which trembled in her hands.

Florence's cheerful voice went on. "We've stirred up the whole machinery here, and the doctors are really counting on us for assistance. I'm telling Sidney how the best of our nurses are attending to hundreds of daily dressings and compound fractures, and giving out medicines at the proper times. Do you remember, when we came here, the orderlies used to give patients the medicines prescribed for the whole day, *all at once?* I do believe that we've succeeded in — " She broke off suddenly at sight of her companion's face.

Selina Bracebridge was looking at her with a stunned expression.

Instantly Florence was at her side. "What is it? What's wrong?"

"This letter from Liz Herbert," said Selina. "It — it seems that Mary Stanley and a party of forty-six nurses will be arriving here — tomorrow."

Florence stared at Selina.

"Mary Stanley!" she exclaimed. "But she has no practical knowledge of nursing. Why would *she* be coming? She helped collect our party in London — but for her to bring out forty-six more women. . . . Selina, I did not ask for more nurses!"

Selina shook her head. "They are not assigned to you, Flo. Liz Herbert says they're to report to Dr. Cumming, at the General Hospital here."

The color drained from Florence's face. There *must* be some mistake. She reached for Liz Herbert's letter and read it, shocked.

How could more nurses have been sent without even

consulting her? Had she somehow been discredited in the eyes of the government? Was the War Office displeased with her work? Was her appointment as Superintendent of Nurses in Scutari withdrawn in this humiliating, public fashion without a word of explanation?

Hurt and bewildered, Florence now wrote Sidney Herbert a long, blistering letter. She reminded him that he had stated in a document made public through the newspapers, that *no additional nurses would be sent out to Scutari until she asked for them.*

She reminded him too of how she had wanted to take with her only a carefully selected group of twenty. Instead, she wrote, "I sacrificed my own judgment and went out with forty females, well knowing that half that number would be more efficient and less trouble. . . ."

This was still such a new and uncertain experiment — having untrained women working among some 3,000 soldiers. So difficult to control them . . .

Flo dipped her pen again and went on writing. "Experience has justified my foreboding. But I have toiled my way into the confidence of the medical men. I have, by incessant vigilance, day and night, introduced something like order into the work of these women. And the plan may be said to have succeeded. . . ."

Wryly, Florence recalled her own happy mood only a short while ago. Her pen moved on, reproaching Sidney Herbert for his thoughtless action. The sending of a "fresh batch of women at no one's requisition, and raising our number to eighty-four. . . ."

Where could they put them? "The quartering of

them *here* is a physical impossibility, the employment of them a moral impossibility. . . ." she wrote. She simply could not take the time now to train these new fe-

males. Past experience led her to believe that the newcomers' total nursing skills would not amount to much. It would be extraordinary good luck if three or four proved really capable. And since she had not been for-

mally removed as the Lady Superintendent, *she* would be held accountable for these women, regardless of who brought them out. Yet Liz Herbert's letter said they were not to report to her! Again the quill raced across the pages.

"You have sacrificed the cause, so dear to my heart," she wrote Mr. Herbert. "You have sacrificed me — a matter of small importance now. You have sacrificed your own written word to a popular cry. . . ."

Florence stared at that last sentence. Hurt and angry though she was, at that moment she began to suspect the possible reason behind this shipment of unwanted nurses. Enthusiastic reports about her mission had been sent to England. One of the chaplains at Scutari, a friend of the Herberts, had written, "As for Miss Nightingale and her companions, nothing can be said too strong in their praise. She works them wonderfully, and they are so useful that I have no hesitation in saying some twenty more of the same sort would be a very great blessing to the establishment. . . ."

The people at home were clamoring for more and better care for their sick and wounded soldiers. They had no idea of the difficulties that Miss Nightingale had to meet, or of the responsibility she had to shoulder when she sent her nurses into the wards.

Sidney Herbert, overworked and pressed on all sides, gave in when Mary Stanley offered her services. Somehow he had agreed to send her. And by having her report to Dr. Cumming, he must have thought it would be less trouble for Florence. This might even have been suggested to him by Mary Stanley, who was undoubtedly jealous of Florence's growing fame, and had no wish to be placed under the Lady Superintendent's authority. Like many other ladies in England, Miss Stanley had rather romantic, impractical notions about nursing the soldiers.

Instead of easing Florence's burden, this arrangement would undermine the authority and respect she had worked so hard to develop. And by casting serious doubts upon her backing from the government, everything she had managed to accomplish so far was in danger of being destroyed.

Florence experienced deep frustration and despair as she waited for the arrival of the Stanley party.

On December 15, 1854, the *Egypt* dropped anchor in the harbor at Constantinople. Shortly thereafter, Charles Bracebridge went on board to see Mary Stanley.

He hoped that their old friendship would help him convince Mary to return to England. If Mary insisted on landing at Scutari, Florence Nightingale would resign. Charles could not bear the thought of this happening. Surely Mary Stanley would understand.

She came to him at once, extending her hand graciously. "Ah, Mr. Bracebridge! How kind of you to escort us to Scutari," she exclaimed. "How is dear Flo?"

"She is quite well," Charles replied, "but terribly overworked." It was the wrong thing to say.

Miss Stanley looked concerned. "The very reason we have come, my dear Charles. We've read all the accounts in the *Times*. Flo has become quite a romantic heroine.

Everyone in London is talking about her. We want to do what we can to help."

Charles gazed at Miss Stanley steadily. He knew she had very little understanding of the work Florence was doing or of the long range results she hoped to gain with it. He tried to explain — but he was no diplomat.

"Flo deserves the admiration," he said. "Actually, the work in the hospital is far from romantic. It's grim, heartbreaking labor. Flo and her nurses endure incredible hardships under terribly crowded conditions. The situation is so bad that I have come to ask you a favor."

Miss Stanley's eyes glowed with pleasure. "My dear Charles, anything at all for Flo."

"Then go back, please. There is no room at the hospital. Our party of forty is crowded into a space of less than five rooms. Our water is rationed. Food is scarce. Flo finds it difficult to supervise the nurses she already has. The best thing you can do for her is go back."

"Go back!" Miss Stanley frowned and up went her chin. "We wouldn't think of it. Surely Flo didn't send you to ask us to return to England!"

Charles shook his head helplessly.

"Well, then!" Mary Stanley shrugged. "Anyway, Flo won't have to bother about us, dear Charles. I intend to supervise my own nurses."

Charles did not give up even then. He warned Miss Stanley of the opposition of the medical officers. He reminded her that Sidney Herbert had given Florence the position of Superintendent of Nurses. Miss Stanley's smile became icy.

"You forget that I came here at Sidney Herbert's request. Can you deny that there is a desperate need for competent nurses here?" she demanded.

Charles could not. Yet *competent* nursing was the key to the problem.

Miss Stanley's party was composed of fifteen nuns, twenty-two paid nurses, and nine ladies. Most of the nuns had no hospital experience, and most of the nurses had not been selected for their high character. As for the ladies, they, like Miss Stanley, had the romantic idea that their mere presence would inspire the soldiers to recover. Charles knew how impossible *they* would find it to deal with the ugly realities of nursing at Scutari. He was certain they would be more trouble than help, and they would confirm the poor opinion the doctors had of hospital nurses.

Discouraged, he left the ship to report to Florence and Selina. Florence had spent hours on her knees dressing wounds. More sick men were arriving from the Crimea. Yesterday there had been two hundred, today many more. The death rate rose steadily.

When Selina saw Charles, she hurried toward him hopefully. He shook his head and Selina knew that he had failed. Mary Stanley was here to stay.

"But there's no room! They will *have* to go back," cried Selina.

"They'll go to the ambassador and he'll provide for them — for now," Charles said. "After all Sidney Herbert sent them."

Florence listened thoughtfully. She had not quite

finished her letter to Sidney Herbert. Tonight, after making her rounds of the wards and corridors she would complete what she had to say to him.

It was after midnight when she took up her pen again. "You must feel that I ought to resign," she wrote sadly, adding that she would remain at her post till he appointed a new Superintendent in her place, "until which time I will continue to discharge my duties as well as I can."

"Shall I post that letter for you, Flo?" Selina asked the next morning.

Florence hesitated. She did not want to leave Scutari. There was so much to be done. She fingered the letter, then put the envelope aside without sealing it. "Not yet," she replied. "Just take the others, please."

Three days later she had not changed her mind about anything in the letter. To make certain that Mr. Herbert would not think she had written in haste, she added a line at the bottom: "Written 15 December. Posted 18 December."

The letter was mailed. It would take nearly two weeks to reach Sidney Herbert — and as long again to hear from him . . .

Miss Stanley and her nurses began almost immediately to cause trouble. When they reported to Dr. Cumming at the General Hospital, he flatly refused to employ them. When they offered to help in the Barracks Hospital, the doctors did not want them either. And when Miss Stanley's group learned of the strict rules

Miss Nightingale had established for all nurses, they rebelled.

"Flo expects entirely too much in the way of discipline," Miss Stanley complained.

It was this very discipline, of course, which had won the medical staff's approval. Now, as Miss Stanley's women began to appear where they were not wanted, the medical officers began to wonder: perhaps allowing "petticoats" into Army hospitals was a mistake after all.

But if Miss Nightingale's influence had suffered a setback in Scutari, her position in England had been considerably strengthened — by Queen Victoria herself. Early in December the Queen wrote to Sidney Herbert:

"Would you tell Mrs. Herbert that I beg her to let me see the accounts she receives from Miss Nightingale and Mrs. Bracebridge, as I hear *no details of the wounded* though I see so many from officers etc., about the battlefield, and naturally the former must interest *me* more than anyone. Let Mrs. Herbert also know that I wish Miss Nightingale and the ladies would tell those poor noble wounded and sick men that *no one* takes a warmer interest or feels *more* for their sufferings or admires their courage and heroism *more* than their Queen. Day and night she thinks of her beloved troops. So does the Prince. Beg Mrs. Herbert to communicate these my words to those ladies, as I know that *our* sympathy is valued by these noble fellows."

The Queen's message arrived shortly before Christmas and the chaplains went through the wards and corridors, reading it to the men. Copies were posted in the hospitals and published in the newspapers. The men were deeply touched.

"To think of *her* thinking of *us!*" a soldier marveled.

"Each man of us ought to have a copy to keep with him till his dying day," said another.

"I only wish I could go and fight for her again," a man with half a leg and his right arm gone whispered hoarsely.

The Queen followed up her message with visible proof of her interest in the men. Bales of gifts arrived for them, along with a personal message for Miss Nightingale. Her Majesty wanted Florence to distribute the gifts herself, as she would know where each item would prove the most useful. Also, the Queen wanted Miss Nightingale to know that *her* goodness and self-devotion in giving of herself "to the soothing attendance upon these wounded and sick soldiers had been observed by the Queen with sentiments of the highest approval and admiration." Would Florence suggest something else the Queen could do for her soldiers?

Yes, there was! For some time now she had been trying to get an increase in the sick pay for the soldiers. She wrote the Queen directly about this, and the result was like a fairy tale: "No sooner said, than done."

In Scutari the astonished officials wondered at the extent of Miss Nightingale's influence. She could get what she wanted straight from the Queen!

During the second week of January 1855, Florence received an answer to her letter. Sidney Herbert acknowledged the mistake he had made in sending Mary Stanley.

He assured Florence that he had meant only to relieve her of some of the wearisome work. Her "experiment" had proved so successful that he felt more nurses would be welcome — especially since there were so many sick and wounded. In the letter he not only reconfirmed her authority but begged her not to resign. Moreover, he left all decisions regarding the Stanley group to Florence's judgment. Mr. Herbert said further, "If you see fit, send Miss Stanley and her party home at my personal expense."

By this time Florence had been able to view the situation more calmly. It might do more harm than good to send the newcomers back — especially since there had turned out to be some excellent nurses among them. Therefore she added some Stanley nurses to her own staff, and sent home several of her own group who had proved incompetent.

At the end of January, Lord Raglan suggested that some of the Stanley nurses be sent to the Crimea. The others, he thought, should go to a new hospital at Koulali, five miles up the Bosporus. Mary Stanley was to organize the nursing staff there. At Koulali, she promptly established the "lady" plan of nursing. Maids were hired to do the disagreeable tasks while the ladies went about the wards cheering up the men and offering pots of tea and delicacies to their favorite patients.

But when the first 300 sick and wounded soldiers were landed, Miss Stanley was at last faced with the reality of filth, infection, and open wounds. She became hysterical, claimed that her health could not stand the strain, and soon left for home.

So the Stanley affair ended with Florence Nightingale more firmly established than ever as the Lady-in-Chief at Scutari. But she had neither the desire nor the time to enjoy her victory. The cruel winter was decimating the British Army. Men fell ill or died by the hundreds. By January 1855, there were 11,000 soldiers in the camp above Sevastopol — and 12,000 in the Army hospitals! Shipload after shipload, the sick arrived at Scutari.

It was, Florence wrote Mr. Herbert, "calamity unparalleled in the history of calamity."

The Lady with the Lamp

In THIS NEW EMERGENCY, everyone turned to Florence Nightingale. She alone appeared calm in the face of disaster. Even the purveyors — the Supply Officers — now came to her, pleading for the supplies she alone could secure without delay.

"Nursing," she wrote Sidney Herbert, "is the least of the functions into which I have been forced."

And yet, despite the staggering load of responsibility, she found time for the nursing too. She had an uncanny way of knowing where she was needed most. And there she went, to comfort a desperately ill new arrival, or perhaps to assist with an amputation. The patient would look up to find the Lady-in-Chief at his side, standing firm, willing herself to witness the pain, willing *him* to bear it, giving new courage and strength to the soldier.

Few soldiers at Scutari died alone. Florence herself must have sat at the bedside of more than 2,000 dying men. She would take down their last words to their families, and promise to help the bereaved wife and children — a promise faithfully kept through Florence's relatives or friends at home. Often Florence provided the financial help.

There was no use telling her to save her strength. Florence Nightingale would spend eight hours on her knees dressing wounds. Or stand for twenty hours supervising the admission of patients, distributing supplies, or, regardless of the dangers of infection, nursing men with typhus and gangrene.

Then the deadly Asiatic cholera again broke out. This epidemic was so virulent that in three weeks seven doctors, three nurses, and old Mr. Ward, the purveyor, had died of the disease.

In this new crisis, Florence Nightingale drove herself mercilessly. Yet even now she managed to write the special reports — some of them thirty pages long — that Sidney Herbert requested. Sitting in her frigid little office, Florence must have worn down hundreds of quill pens as her small, cold hand raced across the pages.

She sent Sidney Herbert a detailed and practical scheme for reorganizing Army hospitals. *She also urged that a Sanitary Commission be sent out from England to inspect the army hospitals and camps.* In spite of all the cleaning and the improved conditions, at the Barracks Hospital in particular, something was terribly wrong. The death rate mounted continuously. . . .

Flo wrote Sidney Herbert, "I work in the wards all day and write all night." Her light was seen burning at all hours. Often her head would drop over her work in utter exhaustion, and then Selina and Charles Brace-bridge would carry her slight form to her narrow bed and cover her. There for a few hours she would sleep like one dead.

The troops adored Florence. "If the Queen was to die," said a victim of the Battle of Alma, "they ought to make *her* Queen, and I think they would."

They thought she would make a good general too. "If *she* was at the head there," they said, "we would be in Sevastopol in a week!"

The men never knew her own troubled thoughts, her weariness, or despair. "She was all full of life and fun when she talked to us," they said, "especially if a man was a bit downhearted."

"Before she came," another veteran reported, "there was cussing and swearing. But after that it was holy as a church." No man would risk offending The Lady's ears.

Florence did not feel it was wise for her nurses to be in the wards after eight at night. Instead, when all was quiet, *she* would make her final tour of the hospital. A new volunteer, who was permitted to go with her once, wrote that it seemed like an endless, but never-to-be-forgotten walk. She and Florence went round the whole of the second story of the huge Barracks Hospital, into many of the wards, and into one of the upper corridors. "As we slowly passed along, the silence was profound," wrote this lady. "Very seldom did a moan or cry from those deeply suffering ones fall on our ears. A dim light burned here and there. Miss Nightingale carried her lantern, which she would set down before she bent over any of the patients. I much admired her manner to the men — it was so tender and kind."

In the long dark corridors, the light of her lamp brought hope to the suffering men.

"Her very presence was like magic," the doctors reported. "The men became heroic for her sake."

One night, as she was about to start on her rounds, Florence was surprised to find a boy sitting outside her door. He appeared to be no more than twelve. When he saw her, he rose unsteadily to his feet. Florence recognized him as Tommy, the drummer boy who had been brought in a few weeks before, suffering from exposure.

"Child, why aren't you in bed?" she asked him.

The lad drew himself up to his full height. "I come to carry the lamp, Lady. Please, I'm strong enough now. I can help you."

He was so bright-eyed and eager that Florence smiled. The child might have a cheering effect on the men too, she thought. "Very well, Thomas. I do need someone to help me with the lamp," she told him. "Thank you for thinking of it." And the tall, slim woman and the boy set out down the long, chilly corridor together.

After that Tommy slept outside the door to the nurses'

quarters. He kept Miss Nightingale's desk lamp and her camp lantern clean and always ready to use.

Thousands of the men in the British Army felt Florence Nightingale's influence. Their letters home were filled with stories about her — and her name became a byword in English homes. One letter became very famous and was passed from hand to hand: "What a comfort it was to see her pass even. She would speak to one and nod and smile to as many more; but she could not do it all, you know. We lay there by the hundreds. But we would kiss her shadow as it fell, and lay our heads on the pillow again, content."

Word of Flo's "influence" on the men reached not only England but elsewhere in the world. Poems and tributes of every kind were written to her. The American poet, Longfellow, wrote the lines which have become the most famous of all:

> Lo! in that hour of misery
> A lady with a lamp I see
>   Pass through the glimmering gloom,
>   And flit from room to room.
> And slow, as in a dream of bliss,
> The speechless sufferer turns to kiss
>   Her shadow, as it falls
>   Upon the darkening walls.

While Florence Nightingale was being idolized in England, the same public furiously blamed the government for the soldiers' plight. As a result of such criticism, there was a change in the government leadership. A new Prime Minister came into office.

Although Sidney Herbert was no longer Secretary of War, the new Prime Minister, Lord Palmerston, was a neighbor of the Nightingales at Embley, and Florence's old friend and supporter. So the new Secretary of War, Lord Panmure, had instructions from the highest source to give every consideration and prompt attention to Miss Nightingale's requests. In England, at least, there were no obstacles to Florence's work. Her reports were forwarded to the Queen as before. And though Sidney Herbert was no longer in the government, he had no intention of giving up his efforts to improve conditions in the Army. He urged Florence to continue to send letters and reports to him. Her suggestions would be forwarded to the proper people.

At the end of February 1855, one of Florence's most important requests was granted. The new Prime Minister sent a Sanitary Commission to the War Zone. The Commission was instructed not only to *investigate* conditions in Scutari and on the Crimea, but to *do* something about them *at once*. And they did! After six months of frustration, everything Florence had pleaded for suddenly began to get done.

The first thing the Commission discovered was the source of the foul stench in the Barracks Hospital — which could be smelled *outside* the walls. Beneath this building there were open sewers and cesspools choked

with filth. The plaster walls were soaked with it. .
decaying mass sent up something much worse than the
smell — a poisonous gas — into every ward and corridor. The water supply was found to be contaminated
too. It was mixed with sewage — and when the channel
was dug up, it was found that the drinking water had
been filtering through the body of a dead horse!

The fact that disease was spread by germs was not yet
discovered. But intelligent people knew that somehow
dirt and foul air spread infection. The filth within the
hospital had been cleared up since Miss Nightingale
had taken charge. But the *air* in the Barracks Hospital
was so sickening that visitors frequently fell ill from
breathing it even for a few minutes! No wonder the
death rate was so high. The wonder was that anyone
survived.

Now the Sanitary Commission engaged an army of
Turkish workers to clean out the sewers, wash the walls
with lime, get rid of the rats and the rubbish that littered the great courtyard and the whole camp surround-
ing the hospital. The hospital was disinfected, and the
water supply purified.

The effect of all this was felt immediately. The death
rate dropped at once. More men recovered from their
illnesses. "The Sanitary Commission," Florence Nightingale said later, "saved the British Army."

And now spring came with a rush, bathing everything
in warm, healing sunshine. Soon there were only 1,100
cases in the Barracks Hospital — and of these, fewer
than 100 were bed-patients.

Florence now had another helper and enthusiastic admirer. This was Alexis Soyer, a French chef, long famous in England. Soyer had come out to Scutari at his own expense and brought with him his black secretary-assistant. Mr. Soyer was dapper, talkative, and full of comic mannerisms. He was also a genius — and Miss Nightingale quickly recognized this. "Others," she wrote a friend, "have studied cookery for the purpose of showy menus . . . he, for the purpose of cooking large quantities of food in the most nutritive and economical manner for great numbers of people."

Although Mr. Soyer was not welcomed by the officials, he came armed with authority to reform the Barracks kitchens — and he set to work at once. He trained soldiers to be cooks — something no one else had done before. He invented ovens and field stoves, and a "scutari teapot" which made and kept hot tea for fifty men. When he appeared in the wards, with his tureens of hot soup or tasty stews, the men cheered.

At long last Florence felt that the Barracks Hospital was in satisfactory condition. She was now able to give her attention to the hospitals in the Crimea. Reports about them were disturbing. The fight for Sevastopol was starting again, and Florence felt keenly the need for better hospital care *close to the front*. Why should the wounded have to suffer the added agonies of going by ship down to Scutari? Florence wanted to improve the diet kitchens in these hospitals with Mr. Soyer's help.

And there was always the problem of discipline among the nurses. The Crimean hospitals had small staffs of women, most of them from the Stanley party. The reports of the behavior of some were upsetting. These women had their own superintendents, who in turn were supposed to be responsible to Florence Nightingale. This was her understanding and certainly what the War Department had intended.

Dr. John Hall was the Chief Medical Officer in the Crimea, but Florence had not yet met him. Dr. Hall was not anxious to meet *her*. She had revealed too many of the weaknesses of the Army hospital administration. Now that the Sanitary Commission had found so many faults, his pride was raw.

Florence had the approval of the War Office for her visit of inspection. But Dr. Hall insisted she had no business in the Crimea. Her appointment, he said, named her "Superintendent of the Female Nursing Establishment in the English Military Hospitals in *Turkey*." The Crimean Peninsula was in Russia. Therefore, Dr. Hall maintained, she had no authority in the Crimea.

Florence was upset by this new opposition, but she did not change her plans. She decided to leave Mrs. Bracebridge in charge at Scutari, and deal with Dr. Hall as best she could.

On May 2, 1855, she sailed from Scutari for Balaclava. She took with her four nurses — including the invaluable Mrs. Roberts. Mr. Soyer and his assistant came on board loaded with kitchen gear. Mr. Bracebridge came, as usual, to help in any way he could, and he brought an invalid soldier, Robert Robinson, to serve as a messenger. Twelve-year-old Tommy, the drummer boy, came too. He called himself "Miss Nightingale's Man" and would scarcely let Florence out of his sight.

Their ship arrived in Balaclava on May 5. Florence noticed that the decks of the many vessels in the harbor were crowded with people, and others were putting out in small boats from the pier.

"Who are they?" Florence asked Charles Bracebridge. "Why have they gathered here?"

Dr. Bracebridge smiled at the modest Lady-in-Chief. "I imagine they've come here for a look at you," he told her.

Florence was dismayed. She did not seek personal glory. She did not want ceremonies and official greetings.

But already various important people were boarding the vessel. Mr. Soyer reported that it soon became a floating reception room, with doctors, senior officers, officials from various departments — including the Sanitary Commission — all crowding around Miss Nightingale. Everyone came who possibly could — except Dr. Hall.

The Captain invited Miss Nightingale to make her headquarters aboard ship.

That afternoon, escorted by a number of important gentlemen, she went ashore to report to Lord Raglan, Commander-in-Chief of the British forces. Florence was provided with a pretty mare to ride, so light brown in color that she appeared golden in the sun. It had been some time since Flo had ridden a horse, but she sat easily in the saddle on her lively mount.

But when the party arrived at Lord Raglan's quarters, Florence learned that he was away for the day. She decided to ride up and see the great guns trained down upon the port of Sevastopol. Many of the soldiers she had nursed in Scutari had come from this very spot.

The sight of a lady, riding a lively mare, and accompanied by so many important gentlemen — some in glittering uniforms — astonished the soldiers. All at once they realized that here was Miss Florence Nightingale herself! Men rushed from their tents to see her — the one person who had brought hope and comfort to them in these months of despair.

Florence was persuaded to sit on one of the cannons so that everyone could catch a glimpse of her. The men cheered her lustily, giving her the traditional British "three times three" salute. *"Hip, hip, hurray! Hip, hip, hurray!"* rang over the high plateau.

Some of the men gathered bouquets of wild flowers that carpeted the plain. They asked her to choose the bouquet she liked best. Florence opened her arms and took them all.

Soon after this she remounted the mare and started down the steep slopes toward Balaclava. Now the strain of the day began to show. Florence's shoulders drooped in exhaustion. Uneasily Charles Bracebridge cantered to her side. "It's nothing, Charles," she said. "Just the unaccustomed fresh air."

Next morning, she began her inspection of the hospitals. Immediately she was met with rudeness. Some of the nurses at the general hospital in Balaclava, encouraged by Dr. Hall's hostility, did not even listen to her instructions.

For the sake of her work Florence could ignore both insolence and rudeness. However, nothing escaped her eyes — the dirt, the careless attitude toward the common soldiers, the disorganized diet kitchens.

Florence realized that she must quickly establish her authority with Dr. Hall. She would see him tomorrow.

But she felt unusually weary the next day — and then, suddenly, she collapsed. Several doctors were summoned and finally a bulletin was issued: Miss Nightingale was ill with Crimean fever — the disease which had killed so many of the soldiers she had nursed at Scutari.

She must be removed from the ship, the doctors advised, and taken to the Castle Hospital on the Heights.

A stretcher was prepared and relays of soldiers volunteered to carry it. Mrs. Roberts walked at Miss Nightingale's side. Mr. Soyer's secretary held an umbrella over Florence's head, to shield her from the sun. Robert Robinson, the invalid soldier-messenger, walked behind, tears streaming down his face. And behind him trailed young Thomas, weeping bitterly because he was neither strong enough for the stretcher, nor tall enough to hold the umbrella for The Lady. But he still carried her lamp, stubbornly refusing to leave it behind on the ship. "She may have need of it yet," he said.

A few days later, word reached Scutari. "She's sick with the fever in Balaclava. They don't think she'll live." No need to ask who "she" was. Sad-faced soldiers told one another the news. The bed-ridden "turned their faces to the wall and cried," a sergeant wrote home.

"All our trust was in her," the men said. "May God spare our gentle Lady with the Lamp."

Angel of the Crimea

FLORENCE hovered between life and death.

"Miss Nightingale's chances for recovery are very poor," her doctor reported. "She is a delicate woman and she has pushed herself far beyond her strength. Indeed, it is remarkable that she has not fallen ill before this."

The sad tidings streaked over the newly built telegraph lines to England. Miss Nightingale was ill . . . dying! It was a national calamity. Grieving people gathered in the streets, waiting for the latest news. At Embley, Parthe and her parents joined the villagers in prayers for Florence's recovery.

Meanwhile, in a hospital hut on the Heights in the Crimea, Florence lay burning with fever. Young Tommy, forbidden to enter the hut, huddled, miserable, outside.

In her delirium, Florence thought the room was full of people demanding supplies from her. Her fever went so high it seemed her frail, wasted form could not survive it. Then suddenly, for the first time in two weeks, Flo fell into a natural sleep.

On May 24, Lord Raglan telegraphed a welcome message to England: Miss Nightingale was out of danger!

She was advised to go home — and she agreed. But to her, "home" was Scutari. And as soon as she regained her strength, she intended to return to the Crimea.

The Lady-in-Chief was put aboard a private steam yacht. The rough passage across the Black Sea and the Bosporus exhausted her so that she was unable to speak or even feed herself. In Scutari, arrangements had been made for her to stay in the chaplain's house. At the pier soldiers were ready to carry her stretcher. Many more waited to greet her and wish her well. When they saw how terribly changed she was, how pale and wasted, they stood in stricken silence, then wept as they followed the slowly moving stretcher up the hill. With a kind of loving fierceness, they fought to carry her baggage.

Her recovery was slow, and it was July before she could even resume her business correspondence. But in August 1855, she was back in her hospital quarters, and at work. She would not spare herself while there was so much still to be done.

During her convalescence Lord Raglan died — of the same terrible fever. Florence knew she had lost a good friend and supporter. The new Commander-in-Chief, General Simpson, was not sympathetic to Florence or to the work of her nurses. There was also a new Senior Medical Officer at the Barracks Hospital — and he took his orders from Dr. Hall.

The other medical officer did not wish to side with Florence against Dr. Hall's man. Even young Dr. McGrigor no longer supported her.

"There is nothing more you can do here," he told her. "The hospital is running smoothly. Your nurses have proved themselves worthy. Why not return to England?"

Flo stared at him in disbelief. "Return! When there's so much more to be done?" How could he not see it!

Dr. McGrigor left her, shaking his head.

One of Florence's concerns was for the soldiers who were well enough to get around but still convalescing. Another was for the soldiers stationed at the camp in Scutari. There was nothing for them to do during their free hours but drink and gamble. Money which should have gone home to their families was spent almost as soon as the soldiers got their pay.

"What can you expect?" the officers told her. "These fellows come from the lowest classes. They are shiftless and ignorant. Most of them cannot even read or write."

Once Florence had retorted. "You vastly underestimate the British soldiers. If we gave them the opportunity to send money home, they would do so. If there were schools and reading rooms for them, they would spend far less time in gambling and drinking."

Florence Nightingale had come to the East to prove the value of women in nursing. Now she had another mission as well — to show the true worth of the British common soldier and to improve his lot.

With her usual efficiency, she began to draw up programs for the education and relaxation of the soldiers.

When her ideas were known in England, people responded at once. A great deal of money was raised and much was accomplished quickly.

Hundreds of cartons containing maps, illustrated books, plays, magazines, and newspapers were sent to the soldiers. Schools were established in the military camps, and schoolmasters were sent out from England.

Recreation was not forgotten. Games of chess, dominoes, football, magic lanterns, and stereoscopes were sent to the soldiers. And Florence opened up a social center. The Inkerman Coffee House was named after one of the famous battlegrounds of the Crimea. Here the soldiers could spend their free time without gambling and getting drunk — and a number of them did.

Until the government took it over, Florence also maintained a money order office. Here she received the money of any soldier who wished to send some part of his pay home. Soon Flo was sending out large sums of money — 1,000 pounds sterling — about $5,000 — a month. Any soldier who promised *her* that he would send money home, *did*. And any soldier who promised *her* he would not drink, *didn't*.

Still uppermost in Florence's mind, however, was her return to the Crimea. There, the hospital kitchens, so carefully planned by Mr. Soyer, were still not built. There too the lack of discipline among the nurses was undermining the program. But Dr. Hall was as hostile as ever, insisting that her authority lay in Turkey, *not* in the Crimea.

In late July, Selina and Charles Bracebridge decided to return to England. They had served Florence faithfully for nine months. Perhaps now they could help her cause better at home.

Florence's family was worried at her being left "alone" so soon after her illness. And so, in September, her Aunt Mai arrived to take the place of Selina Bracebridge.

Aunt Mai was shocked to see her niece so worn, so thin, so pale. She resolved to keep her Flo from working so hard.

But even Aunt Mai was not able to do that. Florence was not only putting in long hours of nursing, she was also keeping up with her enormously increased office work. The stream of people through her door was never ending. She had a much larger nursing staff to direct. (By the time the war ended, she who had been concerned over managing forty nurses, had one hundred and twenty-five under her supervision.)

Aunt Mai helped her niece by copying letters, reports, records. She attended to all the odd jobs Selina used to do. She rose at five and fell into bed at eleven. But Flo, she told the family at home, "writes till one or two, sometimes till three or four."

Florence had a great deal to write about, much to arrange, in the time left to her in the East. A determined attack on Sevastopol had finally routed the Russians, and the seaport was taken in September 1855. The

Crimean War was over — or would be, as soon as the treaty of peace was signed. But that could take many months, and Florence knew *her* work was far from finished.

The sick and wounded still had to be tended properly. It was also important to get her whole nursing staff to work together smoothly. At this last stage, neither the nursing care nor the nurses' morale must be allowed to fall apart. Her mission *must* end as a success. If only the War Office would confirm her position! Then she would not have to fight stubborn officials every inch of the way. . . .

That November her situation in the Crimea was at its worst. But in England her fame was at its height. Returning soldiers sang her praises. Grateful families blessed her in their prayers. The news of her illness, and then of her recovery, and her resolve to remain at her post until the last soldier had embarked for home, elevated her almost to sainthood. People wanted to honor her in every way.

Some of these "honors" were sentimental "biographies" — largely drawn from the writers' imaginations. Reams of poetry, good and bad, were written about her — and sometimes set to music. China statuettes, supposedly of Miss Nightingale, appeared in the shops. There were no portraits of her available — but that did not stop ambitious artists from inventing a "likeness" and selling it.

Streets were named for Florence — ships and even an English race horse!

Thousands of baby girls all over the world were named Florence — sometimes with Nightingale as the middle name. Strangers called on the Nightingale family, asking to see something of hers, or to gaze at the place where *she* had lived — or even just to look at the family of the popular heroine.

Some of her loyal friends at home decided that she might appreciate another kind of tribute — one that would further her work. Vast sums of money were raised "for the training of nurses." And so the Nightingale Fund was born.

When word of the Fund reached the soldiers, they responded by contributing nearly 9,000 pounds — close to $45,000.

Queen Victoria wished to add a personal tribute to Miss Nightingale, to "mark her warm feelings of admiration." Her token was a brooch, designed by Prince Albert especially for Miss Nightingale. This jeweled badge was in the form of a St. George's Cross, in red enamel, surmounted by a diamond crown, with the Queen's royal initials, also in diamonds, below. At the foot of the cross is the word "Crimea," and encircling the cross, the words, "Blessed are the merciful." On the back of the brooch, the inscription: "To Miss Florence Nightingale, as a mark of esteem and gratitude for her devotion towards the Queen's brave soldiers from Victoria R. 1855."

With this handsome decoration came a personal letter from the Queen, written at Windsor Castle, praising Florence for her services in "this great and bloody war

. . . services which are fully equal to those of my brave soldiers, whose sufferings you have had the *privilege* of alleviating in so merciful a manner . . . It will be a very great satisfaction to me, when you return at last to these shores, to make the acquaintance of one who has set so bright an example to our sex."

Deeply touched though Florence was by all this, she wrote Sidney Herbert that the establishment of a training school for nurses from the Fund would have to wait.

And so this large sum of money was put into a bank — while Miss Nightingale, 3,000 miles away, fought death and disease — and Dr. Hall.

Florence was able to return to the Crimea early in October. She was not welcomed.

"There is not an official who would not burn me like Joan of Arc if he could," she wrote Sidney Herbert. "But they know the War Office cannot turn me out because the country is with me."

In the Crimea some of Florence's efforts were bearing fruit. Mr. Soyer's diet kitchens were built and were now feeding hundreds of men. The hospitals were cleaner, and the nursing staffs more efficient.

Then, to her dismay, Florence was recalled to Scutari in November. A new epidemic had broken out. She left with a heavy heart. So much was still undone in the Crimea. What would happen now in her absence?

Return of the Heroine

THE ROOT OF HER PROBLEM in the Crimea, Florence knew, lay in the original wording of her appointment: "Superintendent of the Female Nursing . . . *in Turkey*." Despite her many requests, the War Office had still done nothing to clarify her official position. But now, unknown to Florence, influential people in England were working on her behalf. At long last, Lord Panmure, Secretary of War, was stirred into action.

On March 16, a special dispatch from the War Office arrived in the Crimea. It was so important that the Commander-in-Chief was directed to publish it in the General Orders of the Day. This meant that the dispatch would be posted in every barrack and mess hall on the Crimea — and in Scutari too. No one could possibly avoid reading the sharply worded message or miss its full meaning.

"It appears to me," wrote Lord Panmure, "that the medical authorities of the army do not correctly comprehend Miss Nightingale's position as it has been officially recognized by me. I therefore state briefly for their guidance, as well as for the information of the army, what the position of that excellent lady is.

"Miss Nightingale is recognized by Her Majesty's government as the General Superintendent of the Female Nursing Establishment *of the military hospitals of the army*.

"No lady, or sister, or nurse, is to be transferred from one hospital to another, or introduced into any hospital without consultation with her. . . . The Principal Medical Officer will communicate with Miss Nightingale upon all subjects connected with the Female Nursing Establishment, and will give his directions through that lady."

The Principal Medical Officer was Dr. Hall. The General Order was thus a severe rebuke and a bitter blow to his stiff-necked pride.

For Florence it was a triumph. The struggle for the recognition of her mission was over. If only this authority had come sooner . . .

It was not in Flo's nature however either to look back or to gloat. She arrived in Balaclava on March 24 — in a blinding snowstorm — and was formally welcomed by the Commander-in-Chief. The next day she took her ten nurses to the Land Transport Hospital, where they were badly needed. And then she proceeded to work, as usual.

The Peace Treaty, which officially ended the Crimean War, was signed in Paris on March 30, 1856. On April 29, the good news was announced to the British Army and its allies. One by one, troop ships filled with soldiers sailed for home. One by one, the hospitals were emptied — and closed. The nurses too began to go home in small groups.

Miss Nightingale saw to it that every nurse was provided for. Those who qualified as professional hospital nurses were helped to find suitable positions in England. Many others Florence helped with her own money.

She returned to Scutari at the end of June — to an empty camp. On July 16, 1856, the last patient left the Barracks Hospital. Florence's work there was finished.

Yet she lingered.

Aunt Mai began their packing, casting anxious glances in her niece's direction. The Nightingale family was hoping that their Flo would come home, content at last. Surely she had done enough. Only that morning a letter had come from Mrs. Nightingale, asking, "When will you be coming home, Flo? We must know the exact time and place. Official receptions are being planned . . ."

"Everyone is anxious to meet and talk with you, Flo," wrote Parthe. "You can't imagine how popular you are!"

Florence shrank from public acclaim. The idea of being treated as a national heroine distressed her greatly. Often Aunt Mai would wake in the night to find Flo pacing restlessly.

On one of those sleepless nights, her aunt asked, "What is it, Flo? What's wrong?"

Florence continued to pace back and forth in the pale light of a flickering lamp. She pulled a heavy wrapper about her, shivering, although the air was warm. Then

150

she gazed beyond the windows toward the huge military cemetery where 8,000 British soldiers lay. "Wrong?" she repeated and tears filled her eyes.

"It's over, dearest," her aunt comforted her. "There is nothing you can do to help them now. Come to bed. You must sleep."

"I can't sleep," Florence replied. "Every time I close my eyes I see them. Most of them died needlessly, so needlessly. They did not die of their wounds, Aunt Mai. The war did not kill them."

"What then, Flo?" Aunt Mai's uneasiness was growing.

"Neglect. Indifference. Stupidity. Unsanitary conditions. Inefficiency. Red tape. Lack of proper care." Florence covered her face with her thin white hands. "I see them now. The rows of beds, the horrible suffering. *I can never forget them!*"

It soon became apparent that Florence Nightingale did not intend to rest until she found some way to prevent such a disaster from ever happening again. *She would work to change the organization of army hospitals.* She would fight until she fulfilled what she now believed to be her secret promise to the valiant soldiers she had nursed.

Aunt Mai sighed when she heard of this new task Florence had set herself. She saw that her niece had no intention of returning to England to settle down with her family.

Aunt Mai tried to tell the Nightingales this as tactfully as possible. But Mrs. Nightingale refused to believe it. What more could Florence want? Her daughter was the most famous and popular woman in England! The entire nation was prepared to honor her. There would be parades, bands, speeches, balls — and she and Parthe would be there. A part of it all!

The government did indeed want to bring Florence back in state — aboard a battleship. She declined this honor. Where then would Miss Nightingale first set foot on British soil? Everyone wanted to know.

"The whole regiments of the Coldstreams, the Grenadiers, and the Fusiliers would like to meet Flo," Parthe wrote ecstatically to Aunt Mai. "And failing that, they would like to send their bands to play her home wherever she might arrive, day or night."

No one was told where Florence Nightingale would land in England — or when. Not even her family knew.

Florence and Aunt Mai left Constantinople on July 28, 1856. A Queen's Messenger went with them to attend to such details as their passports and baggage. This much Florence had agreed to. Then she and Aunt Mai embarked for the French port of Marseilles, as Mrs. and Miss Smith. In France, Florence spent a day and a half in Paris, with old friends. Aunt Mai continued on to England.

Thus Florence sailed from France to England alone. The first thing she did when she set foot in England, was to fulfill a promise she had made to the nuns in Scutari. "If I live to return to England, I shall come to you before I see anyone else," she had said.

At eight in the morning she rang the bell at the Convent of the Sisters of Mercy in Bermondsey. She stayed with the nuns for a few hours, and in the afternoon took a train north, still alone — still unrecognized.

Early in the evening, on August 7, 1856, she stepped off the train at the little country station near Lea Hurst, and walked up the steep slope to the manor house.

Mrs. Watson, the housekeeper, adjusting a drape at the front window, saw a lady in a black traveling costume, carrying a small carpet bag, walk slowly up the driveway. Mrs. Watson looked more closely. *"It's Miss Florence!"* she shrieked, and she rushed out to welcome the nation's heroine, home from the war.

Parthe and her parents were only a step behind.

Laughing and crying, Flo embraced them all. "Everything is exactly as I remembered it," she said. She gazed at the wide lawns and gardens, and the high, misty hills beyond. "Best of all," she said to her family, "you are the same."

At this Parthe's tears flowed. *They* had not changed in two years. But Flo looked years older — thin, drawn, and weary, and much, much sadder — even in the gladness of homecoming.

The next day, the peal of the small church bell on the hills and a thanksgiving prayer at the little chapel welcomed Florence Nightingale home. No bands. No shouting and cheering, no speechmaking. It was all the greeting she wanted.

Florence Nightingale's family still fondly hoped that she would consider her work finished, that her reputation and her fame would now content her. They could not understand that she cared nothing about her fame, and that in her reputation she saw only an opportunity for further work.

But for the present Florence needed rest — and Lea Hurst was the ideal place for this. How often she had thought of her hilltop home . . . and remembered the sound of the Derwent River, rushing along its deep valley of red and misty-purple rocks.

She lay on her sofa listening to it now, her eyes closed. The sound recalled to her the roar of the Bosporus.

She moved restlessly, and at once her mother adjusted the shawl spread over her feet. "Rest . . ." she told her daughter.

"Rest . . ." Parthe kept saying.

"Rest, Miss Florence, rest," Mrs. Watson, the housekeeper, murmured each time she came in to straighten up the room.

"Nourishing food and rest — complete rest is necessary to regain your health," the doctors said. It was an endless chorus.

But Florence could neither eat nor rest. She could not empty her mind of the thoughts and plans that churned inside her head. Day after day she lay on the sofa, physically exhausted. At times she found it difficult to breathe. She had fainting spells, and the sight of food made her ill. Yet at night she found the strength to pace the floor of her room, and the sound of the rushing Derwent then was like thunder in her ears.

Florence Nightingale knew that everything she had done in the Crimea would be wasted unless army hospitals — and, indeed, the whole approach to the health and welfare of the soldiers — were reorganized and reformed. Unless the British War Office learned from the terrible fact that 73 per cent of their men had died of neglect in six months, it could happen again. And the men whom Florence had watched die needlessly, would have died in vain. She *must* find a way to have her ideas accepted.

She was faced with two difficulties. She was a woman — and she was a national heroine. She still faced the jealousy of powerful medical men, who felt she had diminished *their* glory. They would oppose anything she proposed. And Florence knew only too well that it was the *men* who made the important decisions in government.

"If I could only find a spokesman," Flo thought, "an influential man to speak for me!"

She wrote to Lord Panmure, the Secretary of War. But he was evasive. "It is more important for you to rest now," he told her.

Then she wrote to Sidney Herbert. Because he was genuinely concerned about her health, he too answered, "Follow the advice of the doctors — don't read, don't write, don't even think."

Florence refused to be put off. In August 1856, she wrote in her private notes, "I stand at the altar of the murdered men and while I live, I fight their cause."

At last, in September, she received some real encouragement. Sir James Clark, an old friend and physician to the Queen, invited her to visit his estate Birk Hall, in the Scottish Highlands. He wrote at the Queen's suggestion, he told Florence. Her Majesty was at Balmoral Castle — only two miles away. The Queen wished to hear of Miss Nightingale's experiences in the East.

Instantly Flo's ills were forgotten. She rose from her sofa. Quickly all her notes and figures and facts were organized, bags packed, good-byes said, and, accompanied by her father, she left for Birk Hall in Scotland, her spirits soaring.

The Nightingale's Magic Power

FLORENCE NIGHTINGALE was asked to visit Balmoral Castle on the afternoon of September 21. That day, as she was driven to the Castle, she recalled her first meeting with the Queen. Florence had been nineteen when she was presented to the equally young Victoria. Now both of them were mature women, and they had something more in common. The Queen knew what it meant to be a woman in a man's world. She had the royal title, Victoria Regina, but little direct power.

Under British law, the Queen could not issue orders of national importance and have them obeyed. Whatever she wanted done by the government had to come through her Ministers and Parliament. But the Queen *could* and *did* use her great influence. Remembering this, Florence relaxed against the cushions of the carriage. She could depend on the Queen.

Florence Nightingale's meeting with Queen Victoria and Albert, the Prince Consort, was an informal one. They talked for more than two hours. The royal pair were charmed with Florence, and deeply moved by her selfless dedication.

That night the Prince wrote in his journal: "She put before us all the defects of our present military system and the reforms that are needed. We are much pleased with her; and she is extremely modest."

Queen Victoria marveled over Florence's genius for organization. "What a clear head!" Her Majesty exclaimed. "I wish we had her at the War Office."

Florence was invited to Balmoral Castle again and again. She went to church with the Royal Family, and she dined with them informally on several occasions. One afternoon, the servants at Birk Hall were astonished to see the Queen drive herself to the manor in a pony cart. She alighted, nodded graciously to the butler and the footmen, who bowed low before her, and asked for Miss Nightingale.

That day she took Florence for a long walk.

There were other visits. Sometimes Queen Victoria spent the whole afternoon with Florence and stayed for tea. She was enchanted with Miss Nightingale and ready to help her cause. By the end of September, Queen Victoria and Miss Nightingale had formed a plan of action.

"You will have to convince Lord Panmure of the necessity for army reform," Queen Victoria warned. "Only he can give an investigating committee official standing. And our Secretary of War is a very difficult man."

Florence smiled. "I've dealt with difficult men before. Most of them can be managed."

There was a twinkle in the Queen's eyes. "So you have learned that lesson too," she said.

Her Majesty arranged a meeting between Florence Nightingale and Lord Panmure at Balmoral Castle on October 5, 1856. A timid person would have been overwhelmed by Lord Panmure's appearance. He was a big man, with a very large head and an enormous amount of hair. He had a way of shaking his head from side to side — and he was known to be stubborn. At the War Office he had been nicknamed "the Bison." It was such a suitable name that Florence had to suppress a smile at their first meeting.

Lord Panmure's sharp eyes seemed to bore through Florence, as if trying to discover just what she wanted for herself. So many people came to him with selfish requests. "The Queen has forwarded to me an outline for army reform," he told her crisply. "*Your* outline, I believe. What more can you tell me about it?"

The burly Scot had come to scoff at Florence Nightingale's ideas. He left under the spell of her charm and intelligence.

With Lord Panmure's approval, a Royal Commission to investigate the reform of army hospitals was organized by January 1857.

The Commission was made up of both military and civilian doctors. Sidney Herbert agreed to act as chairman. He was to be Florence's spokesman, and conduct the public business which she as a woman could not carry on. Florence knew how tactful and wise he was in dealing with difficult people.

It was important now for Florence to be present in London. She took rooms at the Burlington Hotel with her mother and Parthe. There, while Mama and Parthe happily entertained their guests in the drawing room, Florence and the Committee met daily in the small adjoining sitting room. The men jokingly called Florence's sitting room the "little war office," and they referred to her as the "Commander-in-Chief."

The work was exacting, satisfying — and exhausting. Florence had to inspect hospitals and barracks, conduct interviews at distant points, then return home and write out her long reports. Sometimes she had to walk miles through wind and rain — and then miles more along hospital corridors to get the facts for her reports.

Neither Mrs. Nightingale nor Parthe had any idea of the importance of Flo's new interest, though they spoke of her tenderly and wrote about her in fine phrases. At night, when she returned exhausted, they would scold her for not going to parties. It was all too bitterly clear. *They* had not changed, Florence thought wearily. But *she* had.

Well, she no longer craved their sympathy and understanding. Only her work was important now. She had never fully recovered from her Crimean exhaustion — and it seemed to her that she never would. Still, she drove herself and the Commission members hard.

Dr. Sutherland, the sanitation expert who had been at Scutari and Balaclava, said of her, "She is the mainspring of the work. Nobody who has not worked with her daily could know her, could have an idea of her strength and clearness of mind, her extraordinary powers and goodness of spirit. She is one of the most gifted creatures God ever made."

Under Florence's tireless, fiery leadership, the Commission was soon ready to submit its reports to Parliament. If there were no more delays, the reforms proposed by the Commission would soon become laws. British soldiers would never again lack for food, clothing, and medical attention in poorly run hospitals.

At this point Lord Panmure began to hesitate. The Commission's report criticized many officials. He was worried about public opinion, about the reaction of army medical officers, and about his position as Secretary of War. He refused to act.

Florence met him privately. Lord Panmure was stubborn. She saw that more than truth and charm were needed now.

"Do I understand that you refuse to make the work of our Commission official?" she asked him icily.

"My dear Miss Nightingale, it is not a matter of refusal." Lord Panmure threw up his hands.

"What then?" she probed.

"It is a matter of politics. One must move cautiously."

Florence's clear gray eyes narrowed. "Cautiously — or not at all?" she asked.

The "Bison" swayed his head from side to side uncomfortably. "It is difficult for a woman to understand politics," he hedged.

"Not as difficult as you think," Miss Nightingale retorted. "Politics is often a matter of public opinion, is it not?"

The "Bison" nodded.

"Then consider this, sir. If you do not act officially *at once,* I shall publish the complete story of my work at the Barracks Hospital. I shall tell of the neglect, the hopeless confusion, and the unspeakable suffering. What will the effect of public opinion be then?"

Within a month the work of the Royal Commission was made official. This led to the great changes that were eventually made in the care of the English soldiers. As a result of the Commission's work, the living conditions of soldiers throughout the world were improved.

Florence Nightingale was victorious — but once more at the price of her health. In August of 1857, Florence collapsed so completely that even she admitted she was ill. However, she violently refused to be nursed by her family.

"I will go to Malvern," she declared. This was a quiet village in western England, where people went for rest cures.

Parthe offered to go with her, but Florence refused. "I must go alone. I must *be* alone," she insisted. "I have not been alone for four years." Her sudden vehemence frightened Parthe into silence.

When her father visited her at Malvern, he was appalled. Florence appeared to be dying. It was unthinkable that someone from the family should not be with her. Aunt Mai was called — and once again she left her husband and family and rushed to Florence. Aunt Mai never irritated her and never misunderstood her, and Florence responded to her presence.

The stay at Malvern helped her — but this collapse marked the beginning of Florence Nightingale's life as an invalid.

In September, she returned to London and took rooms of her own at the Burlington Hotel. Aunt Mai came to look after her — and to guard her from visitors, "like a dragon," Parthe said. Even she and her mother were asked not to call. Only Mr. Nightingale was allowed to slip in to see Florence. "I shall always be well enough to see *you*," his daughter had written him. Selina Bracebridge too was allowed to come, but other visitors were screened carefully by Aunt Mai and Dr. Sutherland.

The doctors agreed that Florence did not have any specific disease. She was suffering from the exhaustion of almost every nerve and organ in her body. They said her health would never improve, and only constant care and *rest* could prolong her life.

But Florence could not rest unless she worked. Life for her had no meaning without her work. Most recently she had become concerned about the living conditions of the British Army in India — and of the Indian people who lived under British rule. Important officials were begging for appointments with her.

She did see them — one at a time. While these people were with her, they had her fullest attention. She talked with them so briskly and brilliantly, they had no idea of her physical weakness. Afterward, she often fainted. Indeed, her life seemed to hang by a thread, and she, herself, expected to die soon. But she intended to accomplish as much as possible before she did.

She was now writing two books — one on Hospitals, and the other on Nursing. Somehow she managed to write hundreds of pages of closely written notes — as well as hundreds of pages of reports and suggestions to be used by her various committees.

During the summer of 1857, Florence met a handsome widower, Sir Harry Verney. He had admired her work for a long time. Now he became a frequent visitor. He was a member of Parliament and he had supported the reforms Florence worked so hard to put through. Sir Harry fell in love with Florence and asked her to marry him.

Florence had given up all thought of marriage years ago, when she had refused to marry Richard Monckton Milnes. She admired Sir Harry and enjoyed his company — but her work, she explained as gently as she could, still came first. Sir Harry remained her lifelong friend and supporter.

That winter the lonely widower visited the Nightingales at Embley. Eventually he proposed marriage to Parthe — and she accepted. Mrs. Nightingale was delighted. It was an excellent match — even though Sir Harry was much older than Parthe and had four grown children. He was noble and kind and very rich. The excitement of preparing for a wedding pleased Mrs. Nightingale greatly, and the prospect of becoming Lady Verney occupied Parthe completely. The wedding took place at Embley in June of 1858.

In 1859, Florence published her authoritative book, *Notes on Hospitals*. Its influence was worldwide. For the next fifty years few hospitals were built without consulting this book — or Miss Nightingale herself. The Queen of Holland and the Crown Princess of Prussia patiently waited their turn for an appointment with Miss Nightingale. Dukes, ministers, and lords called upon her. The King of Portugal asked her to design a hospital for Lisbon — and her plans were accepted.

All this involved vast correspondence and endless hours of toil from a woman who could scarcely rise from her couch. And yet, some months later, in December of 1859, Florence published another book: *Notes on Nursing*.

The Queen's physician, Sir James Clark, said that this book would do more to promote good health in the home than anything that had ever been written.

In the introduction to this little book, Miss Nightingale stated that her Notes were not intended to teach nurses to nurse. "They are meant simply to give hints for thought to women who have personal charge of the health of others. Every woman . . . has, at one time or another of her life, charge of the personal health of somebody, whether child or invalid — in other words, every woman is a nurse."

This book was an immediate popular success — not only because it was full of practical wisdom, but also because this was the first public word from The Lady with the Lamp since her return from the Crimea. People had no idea of what Miss Nightingale had been doing. It was known that she had gone into retirement. But it was *not* known that the recent upheavals in the War Office and the various army reforms had come through her. Her work behind the scenes of government was always a closely guarded secret.

Now people flocked to buy copies of her *Notes on Nursing*, especially when it was found that here and there she recalled her experiences in the Crimean War. The tone of her writing was gentle, witty, womanly. She was as concerned with preserving family health through cleanliness, good ventilation, and good sanitary conditions as she was in giving sensible directions for the treatment of the sick.

One result of reading the book was that people who feared "the bad night air" began to sleep with their windows open — because Miss Nightingale advised it!

Before the end of the first month, 15,000 copies were sold. Soon *Notes on Nursing* was distributed in factories, villages, and schools. Everyone seemed to be reading it. The little 70-page book was published in many other countries and translated into German, French, and Italian. It was immediately printed in the United States, and reprinted many times. Even today many libraries have copies. The material is fresh and gay — and serious — and still useful.

The tremendous public response to the book once more called attention to the vast Nightingale Fund, collected to help Florence establish a training school for nurses. People wanted to see this Fund put to use.

Florence Nightingale had never lost her concern for

nurses and nursing, but the work for hospital and army reforms had pushed it aside temporarily. Now, once again, plans to found a school of nursing were discussed with her.

Aunt Mai was certain that her niece could not stand the strain of such a project. The members of the committee for the Nightingale Fund were equally certain that no one but Miss Nightingale could carry through this difficult project successfully.

Dismayed, Aunt Mai urged Florence to turn the work over to someone else. "It is less than four years since you returned from the Crimea," she protested. "Yet you have already done enough for several lifetimes."

"But this is something I must do," Florence said. Propped up in bed among her cushions, her eyes grew bright with hope for her lifelong dream — the long-awaited Training School which would raise the position of nurses to the ranks of respected professionals.

The Nightingale School

WHERE TO ESTABLISH the Nightingale Training School? This was the first problem to be solved.

There were many good reasons for deciding on the old St. Thomas' Hospital, near London Bridge. It was large and well managed. More important, the hospital was soon to have a new building in another part of town. Florence would have much to say about its design and equipment.

"When we rebuild," Florence told her co-workers, *"We will add a house for our nurses.* Meanwhile, the hospital has offered us a wing of the present building for our school. Really, the situation couldn't be better."

Her enthusiasm set her to working sixteen hours a day on her plans to equip and set up the training schedule for the "Nightingales." There was no possibility that Florence could take charge of the school in person. She could leave her couch only for short periods, and could scarcely stand alone. So finding the right Superintendent for the student nurses of the Nightingale Training School was of utmost importance. And here again she was in luck. When Florence interviewed the Matron of

St. Thomas' Hospital, she found her to be exactly the sort of person her school required.

Mrs. Wardroper was a small and energetic lady of immense dignity and indisputable authority. At forty-two she had been left a widow with small children. Rather than become a genteel poor relation in the family, Mrs. Wardroper struck out independently and became a nurse. It was an attitude and a situation Florence could understand.

"I don't suppose your relatives approved of your decision," she remarked drily.

Mrs. Wardroper had led a hard life, but it had not spoiled her sense of humor. She smiled. "You might put it that way. But it was something I wanted to do. In fact, *had* to do —and with no school to teach me."

The words were familiar.

Florence liked the Matron's belief in discipline and her high ideals for the nursing profession. Together they would make the Nightingale Training School a success.

Although Mrs. Wardroper was enthusiastic, she was also realistic. "We must be prepared for harsh criticism," she told Florence.

"I have never been seriously wounded by criticism," Florence said lightly.

"Some will come from within the hospital itself," the Matron pointed out. "You are, of course, familiar with Dr. South's views."

Florence certainly was. The Senior Surgeon of St. Thomas' had written some *Observations on Training Establishments for Hospitals*. Nurses, he said, learned by experience and they needed only the simplest instructions on how to make poultices and beds. "Ward maids" were, after all, in the same position as house maids.

"We shall just have to prove Dr. South wrong," Florence declared. "Absolutely wrong."

In May of 1860, the first advertisements for applicants to the Nightingale Training School appeared in the newspapers. Fifteen young women were selected to begin training on July 9, 1860.

Every detail of their schooling, conduct, and housing had been carefully thought out. For the first time there was such a thing as a Nurses' Home. Each of the probationers, or "probies," as the student nurses were called, had a bedroom of her own. There was also a sitting room to be shared by all. Florence had provided this with books, pictures, and vases. She planned to have flowers sent down regularly from Embley. Unable to leave her bed, Florence depended on trusted friends to see that her wishes were carried out.

Escorted by Mrs. Wardroper, Selina Bracebridge made a tour of inspection of the Nurses' Home on an upper floor of St. Thomas' Hospital. She viewed the nurses' quarters with considerable interest — and perhaps with vivid recollections of the dismal nurses' Tower in Scutari.

"This is so attractive and comfortable," Selina said.

Mrs. Wardroper agreed, but appeared doubtful about the "extras" insisted on by Miss Nightingale. "I feel we may spoil the girls with such comforts," she said.

"They cannot expect all this when they leave us for actual hospital positions."

Florence had no intention of spoiling her young nurses, but she believed that pleasant surroundings were an aid to well-being. They were not to scrub and scour and waste their energy in being house maids. But she expected them to work hard.

The girls were required to rise at six, work all day long — and at night to write up their notes for the day. They washed patients, made beds, assisted the ward nurses, and received instruction from the most experienced Sisters, as head nurses were called in England. The probies were required to serve meals to the patients and feed those who needed help. For their own meals they were allowed half an hour, with fifteen minutes for getting to and from the dining hall.

When the house physicians arrived, the probies were divided into small groups and made the rounds with them as they examined the patients. They had to observe each patient carefully and write out reports on each one. With the surgeons, they were taught to change dressings, and told about the special care of surgical patients.

In the afternoons, lectures by visiting doctors were given on anatomy, diseases and their effect on the body, and on many other subjects that Florence had longed so vainly to learn when she was a girl.

The probationers did have short periods of rest during the day. And there was tea at five, which revived them somewhat and kept them going until about nine at night. By that time all the patients were ready for the night.

Back in their rooms the probies would have dearly loved to collapse on their beds — but one more duty awaited them. The notes — required of them by Miss Nightingale and Mrs. Wardroper.

When the probationers had time to relax in their sitting room, they often talked about the problem of meeting Miss Nightingale's standards.

Notes on everything — just everything! "Every tiny detail," complained one dark-haired miss. "I don't know if I can get it all down. I have never done so much writing in my whole life!"

"Nevertheless, you had better try," advised a more serious-minded probie. "Be especially careful to keep everything up-to-date. Mrs. Wardroper said she might call for our notebooks at any time. She meant it!"

"Oh, glory!" cried the first girl. "Do you think Miss Nightingale will see them too?"

"I wouldn't doubt it. She read our last examination papers. She manages to keep an eye on everything we do."

"Oooooh!" the little probie wailed and glanced around as if she half-expected to see eyes staring at her from the walls. And then she fled to her room and her notebook.

A tall, pretty girl, looking out of the window, called to the others in the sitting room. They all watched as two probationers left by the front door of the hospital. The girls walked close together, sedately following the hospital rule that no probationer was ever to go out alone. But as they reached the corner, the girls separated and shot off in different directions.

Everyone in the sitting room laughed. This was something they all did when they had time off — always hoping their sin of separation would not be observed by Mrs. Wardroper.

The strict rules were necessary for these high spirited young women who were pioneers in *trained* nursing — a word Florence Nightingale used to describe the profession. It was the word *trained* that was destined to make a world of difference in the public image of the hospital nurse. Meanwhile, people in London were following with interest the progress of the Nightingale probationers. Some of the medical men were certain that women could never learn anything useful about anatomy and disease. Accustomed to the common, tipsy frumps of that period, they simply would not believe that Miss Nightingale's methods could produce intelligent nurses of the highest character, ideals, and trained skill.

Florence was equally convinced that she could do just that. She believed there were two ways to accomplish it. First, by careful selection of probationers, and second, by rigid enforcement of the school rules.

A constant check was kept on each girl. The Matron sent Florence detailed monthly reports. In addition, Mrs. Wardroper wrote long, confidential, personal reports on the student nurses.

For all the strict discipline, the probationers led a

pleasant life. They worked hard, but they learned much. It was becoming increasingly clear that the Nightingale nurses were vastly different from the slovenly women who staffed the ordinary hospitals. Flo's girls wore a uniform — something taken for granted today, but quite new then. They wore brown dresses and snowy caps and aprons. A magazine writer said they: "looked like bits of extra light as they moved cheerfully and noiselessly from bed to bed."

This favorable description received much attention. Mrs. Wardroper began to get requests for Nightingale nurses from many parts of the country. When the first class graduated at the end of the year, a wide choice of positions was open to the girls. Thirteen of the original fifteen probies received their Certificates. Six of these stayed on at St. Thomas' Hospital.

As probationers they had been supplied with room, board, laundry, and uniforms by the Nightingale Fund. They were also given about $50 in spending money during their one year of training. Those who worked in hospitals for a year after becoming "Certificated Nurses" received an additional sum of money. Florence Nightingale expected her nurses to continue in hospital work, and by their example, to help reform poor conditions wherever they went. In time, she hoped that her girls would become teachers and even superintendents in other training schools. Her trained girls were meant to be leaders, and most of the Nightingales did not disappoint her.

At the end of the first year, the school was judged a

tremendous success. Now there were more applicants than could be handled. Florence began to look forward to the time when the school would be enlarged in the hospital's new quarters.

But the bright triumphant summer turned suddenly dark. On August 2, 1861, Florence's dear friend Sidney Herbert died.

Everything she had accomplished had been done with his aid. Now, without him, she felt lost. She did not know if she could continue to work at all.

It was the Civil War in America that brought Florence out of her grief. The war had been declared in April, 1861. In October, President Lincoln's Secretary of War appealed to Florence for help in organizing hospitals for the American soldiers. The conditions described there reminded Florence of the sickening disorder and misery she had found in Scutari. Once again she saw before her row upon row of desperately sick and wounded men. She relived the horror of death through neglect. And once again Florence Nightingale moved into action.

A Woman's Central Association of Relief had been formed in New York, she learned. Female nurses were being allowed to enter the Northern military hospitals — because Florence Nightingale had proved it could be done. But now these volunteers needed help — advice on such matters as proper diet and cooking techniques.

Soon Flo's pen was flying across the pages, this time for the benefit of the United States.

The Nightingale Nurses

THE BUILDING of the new St. Thomas' Hospital occupied much of Florence Nightingale's attention for several years. Even though she could not watch over the work personally, she was consulted about every detail of its construction and equipment.

By October of 1865 she was settled in a house of her own, at No. 10 South Street, in the West End of London. It was from this house that she continued to "arrange things," as she called it, for the rest of her long and remarkable life. Here she became *the* authority on special problems and Indian matters for the British Government. Engineers, supply officers, medical men — everyone concerned with that far-flung corner of the British Empire, wrote to her for advice. It became the custom for every newly appointed Viceroy of India to pay a visit to Miss Nightingale before leaving England.

At the same time, Florence continued to use her influence for reform in laws to help the poor, improve conditions in work houses and insane asylums, and to change laws concerned with the right of women to own property. On all these matters she could always quote facts and figures to prove that reforms were necessary. Her friends said that Flo read such facts the way other people read novels.

Her vast knowledge made her a force to contend with. But how much or how little she was able to influence the government, depended on politics — on who was in office, and on which men in the Cabinet were in favor of reform. When the forward-looking men were out of office, Florence felt that *she* was "out of office" too, for then her influence was greatly lessened and she was quite discouraged. At such times she felt most keenly — though she still worked ten to sixteen hours a day — that she was not doing enough.

It was during one such period of gloom that a friend whom she greatly respected, wrote her: ". . . you work on in silence, and nobody knows how many lives are saved by your nurses in hospitals (you have introduced a new era in nursing): how many thousand soldiers are now alive . . . owing to your forethought and diligence . . . how many natives of India (they might be counted probably by hundreds of thousands) have been preserved by the energy of a sick Lady who can scarcely rise from her bed. . . . But I know it and often think about it, and I want you to, so that in later years . . . you may see what a blessed life yours is and has been. . . ."

In 1871 the *new* St. Thomas' Hospital was at last completed. Queen Victoria, herself, opened the hospital on a bright June day — and the Nightingale Training School was moved into its new quarters.

The excellent Mrs. Wardroper remained its Superintendent — a post she held for 27 years — but Flo became the active head of the School and the Chief of the Nightingale Nurses.

With the school so much larger now, Florence engaged an Assistant Superintendent, called the Home Sister. This lady encouraged the students to read and study, to listen to music, and to go to church. The Nightingale Nurses were to be well-rounded, educated women.

Because they were to be "trained to train" others, they were also encouraged to be more patient and tactful. Florence had discovered that frequently her graduates, proud of their new "trained" skills, considered *their* way of doing things the *only* way and the *best* way. Florence knew that this could only create antagonism, not bring about reforms. Her nurses must obey existing authority, and follow the rules of the institutions to which they were sent. Conditions in many institutions were still dreadful, but the people in charge must come to believe in the new way, if real change was to take place.

It was hard to teach this to the impatient young pioneers in modern nursing, but Florence would often emphasize the point by recalling her own experiences and frustrations in Crimea: "Do you think," she asked one discouraged nurse, "I should have succeeded in doing anything if I had kicked and resisted and resented? . . . I have been shut out of hospitals into which I had been ordered by the Commander-in-Chief, obliged to stand outside the door in the snow until night, have been refused rations for as much as ten days at a time for the nurses I have brought by superior command. I have been as good friends the day after with the officials who did these things — have resolutely ignored these things *for the sake of the work.*"

Florence became personally acquainted with every "probie" as soon as the nurse's trial period was completed. This meant a visit and an interview with the Lady-in-Chief herself. Many a probie grew faint with fright at the prospect, but usually emerged from the encounter starry-eyed and determined to please Miss Nightingale in *everything.*

As soon as the door closed on a girl, Florence wrote a vivid character sketch of her.

"Miss C——. A most capable little person . . . seems as good as can be. No complaints . . . enthusiasm for her work . . . and for the Sisters. Likes the bustle and hard work of Surgical Ward . . ."

Or, "Miss H——. Tituppy, flippant, pretension-y . . . Ambitious, clever, not much feeling. Talk-y . . ."

"Miss V——. More cleverness than judgement, more activity than order, more hard sense than feeling, never any high view of her calling, always thinking more of appearance than of the truth . . ."

"Miss G——. A woman of good feeling and bad sense . . . She wants a very steady hand over her . . ."

Each girl's file contained the character sketch, along

with results of examinations — letters and comments sent by the Matron and the Home Sister. Florence invited the students to comment on their lectures and their work. If a just complaint or a good suggestion was made, Florence followed it up promptly.

Each nurse who graduated from the Nightingale Training School was like a missionary who went forth to teach new ideas. Florence therefore carefully studied each girl's file so that her graduate nurses would be placed in posts where they would do the most good. Since she never lost track of any of her nurses, each file continued to grow through the years.

When one of her graduate nurses went to a new post, Florence saw to it that flowers and a fond letter were sent ahead to welcome her. If it was a long journey, someone was waiting at the train with a basket of lunch.

If a nurse became ill, she was sent special diet foods. If she needed rest, or a change, she was sent to the country or the seaside at Miss Nightingale's expense.

A nurse or matron who was overworked might be invited to No. 10 South Street for "a Saturday to Monday in bed," with Florence's housekeeper to care for her needs.

In June of 1873, Florence wrote: "I am immersed in such a torrent of my trained matrons and nurses, going and coming, to and from Edinburgh and Dublin, to and from watering places for their health, dining, tea-ing, sleeping — sleeping by day as well as by night . . ." But this was the kind of "immersion" Florence loved best. From it she drew new strength and energy for her school and for her "daughters," her nurses.

Gradually other schools were established — often under the direction of Florence's ablest nurses. By 1880, most of the important nursing posts in England were filled by Nightingale nurses. They were the Matrons and the Superintendents in the major hospitals and institutions not only in the British Isles, but also in Canada, the United States, Sweden, Germany, India, Ceylon, and Australia.

Wherever a Nightingale nurse went, her Lady-in-Chief went with her in spirit, through messages of encouragement and guidance, and heartwarming little gifts.

The success of her school and of her nurses had a healthful effect on Florence. Occasionally, her brother-in-law, Sir Harry Verney, would persuade her to go driving with him in the London Parks. Now and then she was even able to stroll along the paths, leaning upon his strong arm.

These outings had to be kept a secret from the general public. The Lady of the Lamp was a beloved legend. Sometimes in theater crowds, or on the streets, some pale lady in black would be mistaken for Miss Nightingale. Immediately she would be surrounded by an excited crowd, with people begging to touch her hand or her shawl or her gown. Florence had no wish for this kind of notice.

The Nightingale Training School had been in existence for twenty-two years — but Florence had never actually seen it. On January 27, 1882, Florence Nightingale paid her first and only visit to the new St. Thomas' Hospital. She inspected the quarters of the training school and one of the hospital wards. It was all exactly as she had pictured it — as she had *directed* it to be.

Florence was satisfied with her school and the course of training for her nurses, but she knew they must never stop learning.

Great discoveries were being made in medicine. Anesthetics were now commonly used to control pain. Antiseptics were used to control infections. New kinds of surgery were now possible — and this was only a beginning. Florence foresaw even greater advances — and she also realized that *nurses* would have to keep pace with the progress made by the doctors.

In a talk which she prepared for her pupils, she said, "For us who nurse, our nursing is a thing in which, unless we are making *progress* every year, every month, every week — take my word for it, we are going *back*. The more experience we gain, the more progress we can make. The progress you make in your year's training with us is as nothing to what you must make every year *after* your year's training is over. A woman who thinks, 'Now I'm a full nurse, a skilled nurse, I have learned all that there is to be learned' does not know what a nurse is, and she will never know. She is gone back already."

The Nightingale nurses called their Chief's messages

"trumpet calls to duty" and few remained unmoved by them.

In 1887, Queen Victoria celebrated her Golden Jubilee — her fifty years on the throne of the British Empire. Privately, Florence considered this her Jubilee year, also. Fifty years before, in February of 1837, *she* had received a Call to service — and she had answered it to the best of her ability.

The Last Years

Florence Nightingale, who had at one time thought that she would never see her fortieth birthday, outlived all of her immediate family and her closest friends. On her seventy-fifth birthday, May 12, 1895, she wrote, "I have lost much in failure and disappointments, as well as in grief, but do you know, life is more precious to me now. . . . Life is a splendid gift!"

She made the most of every moment, for "the last years of life were and ought to be the best," she said. Year after year, she was able to write happily to one friend or another: "I have my hands full and am not idle. . . . *I am soaked* in work!"

Gradually, Florence's strength ebbed. After 1896, she never left her South Street bedroom. Yet her mind remained clear and active as ever, and her interest in all her projects remained keen.

She continued to carry on her huge correspondence with her nurses, matrons, and superintendents at all their far-flung posts. Important people from all over the world still sought her advice and waited patiently for a chance to see her in person.

A housekeeper now lived with Florence and had charge of her house. One of the Nightingale nurses was also engaged to care for Florence, which Florence said was nonsense. *She did not need a nurse.* Frequently, after the nurse had tucked her in for the night, Florence would somehow find the strength to go to the nurse's bed and tuck *her* in!

Suggestions from Flo's book, *Notes on Nursing,* were now used in her own care as an invalid. Pets, she had said, "helped to cheer a patient." Hers now included six cats. Many of her notes and letters bore mysterious little smudges, which on closer inspection proved to be cat-paw prints over fresh ink.

Young nieces, nephews, and cousins were welcome visitors. One of them, the young Sir Harry Verney, said she was his "favorite and perfect aunt." Florence was never too busy nor too tired to listen to their problems, to exclaim over examination papers, or to listen to confessions of first love, or young heartbreak.

Her private life was so carefully guarded, that long before 1897, most people thought the heroine of the Crimea was dead. But in 1897, at the Diamond Jubilee for Queen Victoria — to celebrate her sixty years on the throne — there was an exhibition to show the tremendous progress of nursing during the Victorian era. This was planned around Florence Nightingale and her heroic, pioneering work, and she was asked to provide some personal things for it. As usual Florence was reluctant "to go on public display." Finally she allowed a portrait and a bust of herself to be shown. Then someone found her old Crimean "carriage" at Embley. That was brought down, and of course her lamp.

Excitement ran high as people thronged to see these possessions of The Lady who had become such a legend in her own lifetime. The old soldiers Florence had once nursed in the Crimea gazed at her things as if they were sacred.

"Think of that! The Lady ain't dead!" they told one another as they went up to kiss the carriage and gaze at the lamp. Someone brought fresh flowers every day and decorated Miss Nightingale's statue with them. When she heard of it, she said she didn't like any of this — *not at all.*

The true fruits of the Crimean War, she said, were the tremendous lessons learned from the tremendous blunders. And the beginning of trained nursing, which was made possible afterward.

For Florence, the occasion was one for giving thanks to God — for "the immense blessings I have had, the longings of my heart accomplished."

On August 13, 1910, Florence Nightingale fell asleep at noon — and did not wake again. She had lived ninety years and three months.

In accordance with her wishes, she was buried in the churchyard at East Wellow, near Embley, beside her father and mother. There is only the simplest of inscriptions on the fourth side of the family tombstone: *F.N. born* 1820. *Died* 1910.

Epilogue

The Lamp Burns On

FLORENCE NIGHTINGALE is chiefly remembered for the two years she spent in the Crimea — a short time in her long and productive life. But those were critical years, for it was during the ordeal in Crimea that she was first able to test her ideas on trained nursing. And it was through her work in the Crimea that she won the fame which made her later work possible.

Every soldier in the world owes a debt of gratitude to Florence Nightingale. For it was she who started the far-reaching reforms that still affect his health and well-being.

The International Red Cross grew out of the inspiration she gave to the Swiss gentleman, Henri Dunant. He said it was her work in the Crimea which inspired him to start the Red Cross movement.

District nursing, established for the care of the sick and poor in their own homes, was also inspired by Florence Nightingale. This grew into the Visiting Nurses Organization which we know in the United States.

But her greatest contribution was in the field of hospital nursing — and the career opportunities it has opened for women.

Florence Nightingale, of course, did not *originate* nursing. What she did was found *modern nursing,* with its use of special training and knowledge. Because of her special knowledge and dedication, what she demonstrated was nursing as an art and a respected profession.

The influence of the Nightingale Training School was worldwide. Several such nursing schools were soon established throughout the United States. In 1889, Miss Louisa Parsons — a much honored graduate of the Nightingale School — came to the United States as a Superintendent of the new training school for nurses in the University of Maryland Hospital in Baltimore. Miss Parsons arrived with a new uniform for nurses, designed by Miss Nightingale. This was a gray-and-white-striped cotton dress, white apron with a square bib, black stockings and black, high-topped shoes. She also brought with her the gift of a lovely, fluted lace cap — to be awarded to the students when they finished their probation period. Thus the Maryland School of Nursing inherited the Nightingale cap — an honor of which its nurses are still very proud.

By 1910 there were more than one thousand Training Schools for Nurses in the United States alone. All were the outgrowth of Florence Nightingale's work. In May of that year, a huge meeting was held in New York City to honor the fiftieth anniversary of the first Nightingale

189

Training School in London — and "to testify to the admiration of the entire American people for Florence Nightingale's great record and noble life."

The Nightingale School is still part of St. Thomas' Hospital in London. It now graduates about 120 "Nightingales" a year. It still remains true in spirit to the intentions of its founder. The professional qualities and the bedside skills which Florence Nightingale required of her nurses are, if anything, in greater demand today than they were in her lifetime.

Florence Nightingale made of nursing a noble profession, and stamped her own image on it. "Nursing is an art," she said, "and if it is to be made an art, it requires as exclusive a devotion, as hard preparation, as any painter's or sculptor's work; for what is having to do with dead canvas or cold marble compared with having to do with the living body — the temple of God's spirit."

Florence Nightingale's Lamp burns as bright as ever, as thousands of young nurses symbolically light their candles from it at their graduation ceremonies. All nurses, when they graduate, also recite a solemn pledge. Many of them believe that they are speaking Florence Nightingale's own words. But Florence never exacted any vows from her nurses. This pledge reflects not her words but her ideals for the nursing profession. And, although it was composed in the United States, the pledge has linked nurses the world over, for it has been translated into many languages. Nurses today would feel "ungraduated" if the Nightingale Pledge were to be left out of their closing ceremonies.

Florence Nightingale, who wanted no monuments, lives in these words:

I solemnly pledge myself before God and in the presence of this assembly, to pass my life in purity and to practice my profession faithfully. I will abstain from whatever is deleterious and mischievous, and will not take or knowingly administer any harmful drug. I will do all in my power to maintain and elevate the standard of my profession, and will hold in confidence all personal matters committed to my keeping and all family affairs coming to my knowledge in the practice of my calling. With loyalty will I endeavor to aid the physician in his work, and devote myself to the welfare of those committed to my care.*

With every candle lit for the graduating ceremony, Florence Nightingale's Lamp glows brighter.

* The Nightingale Pledge was drawn up at the old Harper Hospital in Detroit, Michigan, and was first used by its graduating class in the spring of 1893. Quite fittingly, it is an adaptation of the Hippocratic Oath taken by physicians.